GOLIATH STRIKES BACK

HOW TRADITIONAL RETAILERS ARE WINNING BACK CUSTOMERS FROM ECOMMERCE STARTUPS

Peter S. Cohan

Apress®

Goliath Strikes Back: How Traditional Retailers Are Winning Back Customers from Ecommerce Startups

Peter S. Cohan
Management Division, Babson College, Wellesley, MA, USA

ISBN-13 (pbk): 978-1-4842-6518-5
ISBN-13 (electronic): 978-1-4842-6519-2
https://doi.org/10.1007/978-1-4842-6519-2

Managing Director, Apress Media LLC: Welmoed Spahr
Acquisitions Editor: Shiva Ramachandran
Development Editor: Rita Fernando
Coordinating Editor: Rita Fernando

Cover designed by eStudioCalamar

Distributed to the book trade worldwide by Springer Science+Business Media New York, 1 New York Plaza, New York, NY 100043. Phone 1-800-SPRINGER, fax (201) 348-4505, e-mail orders-ny@springer-sbm.com, or visit www.springeronline.com. Apress Media, LLC is a California LLC and the sole member (owner) is Springer Science + Business Media Finance Inc (SSBM Finance Inc). SSBM Finance Inc is a **Delaware** corporation.

For information on translations, please e-mail booktranslations@springernature.com; for reprint, paperback, or audio rights, please e-mail bookpermissions@springernature.com.

Apress titles may be purchased in bulk for academic, corporate, or promotional use. eBook versions and licenses are also available for most titles. For more information, reference our Print and eBook Bulk Sales web page at http://www.apress.com/bulk-sales.

Any source code or other supplementary material referenced by the author in this book is available to readers on GitHub via the book's product page, located at www.apress.com/9781484265185. For more detailed information, please visit http://www.apress.com/source-code.

Printed on acid-free paper

To Robin, Sarah, and Adam.

Contents

About the Author

Peter S. Cohan is Lecturer of Strategy at Babson College where he teaches strategy and entrepreneurship to undergraduate and MBA students. He is the founding principal of Peter S. Cohan & Associates, a management consulting and venture capital firm. He has completed over 150 growth-strategy consulting projects for global technology companies and invested in seven startups – three of which were sold for over $2 billion. Peter has written 15 books and writes columns on entrepreneurship for *Forbes* and *Inc.* Prior to starting his firm, he worked as a case team leader for Harvard Business School Professor Michael Porter's consulting firm. He has taught at MIT, Stanford, Columbia University, New York University, Bentley University, the Vienna University of Technology, Tel Aviv University, and the University of Hong Kong. Peter earned an MBA from Wharton, did graduate work in computer science at MIT, and holds a BS in electrical engineering from Swarthmore College.

Acknowledgments

This book would not have been possible without the help of many people. My colleagues at Babson College – including Nan Langowitz, Danna Greenberg, JB Kassarjian, Allan Cohen, Sam Hariharan, and Keith Rollag – provided me with very helpful support and suggestions for improvement.

I am also grateful to the many people who offered me their views on the topics discussed in this book including Harvard Business School Associate Professor, Laura Huang; Stanford Business School Professor, Charles O'Reilly; Yale School of Management Lester Crown Professor of Leadership Practice, Jeffrey Sonnenfeld; Academic Director of Wharton's Baker Retailing Center, Thomas S. Robertson; MIT Sloan School Senior Lecturer, Sharmila Chatterjee; Northeastern University Associate Professor of Journalism, Dan Kennedy; Director of University of Colorado Boulder's News Corp, Chuck Plunkett; and author Marc Levinson.

Many analysts were also very helpful. These include Tory Gundelach, VP of Retail Insights at Kantar Consulting; Charlie O'Shea, retail analyst at Moody's; and Jonathan Matuszewski, analyst at Jefferies. Executives and investors – including Chris Lynch, CEO of AtScale; Ben Gordon, Managing Partner, Cambridge Capital; Michael Greeley, General Partner, Flare Capital Partners; and Santi Subotovsky, General Partner, Emergence Capital – also shared their valuable insights.

Finally I deeply appreciate the help of Rita Fernando and the team at Apress for ably bringing this book to fruition.

Preface

I wrote this book to answer questions that have puzzled me for decades: why do so many successful companies cling to the past instead of creating the future? Are all such incumbents doomed to stagnate, decline, or implode because they can't adapt effectively to the threats and opportunities created by changing technology, upstart competitors, and evolving customer needs? If not, what can incumbents do to grow faster?

I explored these questions in two of my earlier books, but I now realize that until about 20 years later, I was missing a critical piece of the puzzle. For example, in *The Technology Leaders*[1] – inspired by my first consulting project aimed at answering these questions for the R&D department of a leading Asian telecommunications company – I studied companies that had prevailed in more than one wave of new technology. Four specific organizational attributes distinguished them from other companies:

- **Entrepreneurial leadership:** The ability to hire and motivate entrepreneurs to work for the company
- **Open technology:** A willingness to develop technologies from sources other than a company's own R&D department – for example, through acquisitions or partnerships
- **Boundaryless product development:** Developing new products by coordinating functional departments such as engineering, marketing, manufacturing, and sales – to collaborate with early-adopter customers
- **Disciplined resource allocation:** Shifting resources from unsuccessful projects to more promising ones in a disciplined manner

Looking back on this framework, I now realize that I missed an important point – the CEOs of the most successful high technology companies had very different mindsets than the less successful companies. For example, Microsoft at the time was led by Bill Gates, a CEO who had founded the company, and Cisco Systems' CEO, John Chambers, excelled as an acquirer

[1]Peter S. Cohan, "The Technology Leaders: How America's Most Profitable High-Tech Companies Innovate Their Way to Success" (Jossey-Bass, 1997).

of new technologies that the company's customers wanted to buy. Simply put, when I wrote *The Technology Leaders*, I was under the illusion that to persuade leaders to adopt these organizational attributes, it would be sufficient to provide case studies of how these principles led to superior performance. From my current perspective, I did not delve enough into how a CEO's mindset might cause them to view the cost of putting these ideas into practice as far outweighing the benefits.

I tackled this question again in my 2000 book, *e-Profit*,[2] when I challenged the prescription in Clayton Christensen's book, *The Innovator's Dilemma*,[3] that companies should set up a separate subsidiary to kill the parent company with a disruptive technology. I argued that companies would starve such subsidiaries of capital and talent and would ultimately dissolve them to cut costs in an economic downturn. I presented case studies intended to show that CEOs should lead a business model transformation from the old technology to the new one.

My conclusion was that different firms respond to change – be it disruptive technologies or shifting market conditions – differently. I suggested that the success of ecommerce initiatives in creating change depends on two factors:

- **The source of the ecommerce strategy:** Is the ecommerce strategy coming from internal experimentation or as a response to an external threat?
- **The extent to which the ecommerce strategy alters the firm's business model:** Does the ecommerce strategy complement the existing business model, or does it force the firm into an entirely new way of doing business?

I now realize that the companies I highlighted as successes were led by entrepreneurs who had taken their companies public. The less successful adopters of ecommerce were run by CEOs who had risen to leadership by applying strategies that worked effectively before the Internet was available for businesses and individuals. Such CEOs, I now realize more clearly, were in the grip of confirmation bias – lapping up information that reinforced their belief that ecommerce would be a flash in the pan rather than a significant force to which they would need to respond. Viewed in this light, I realized that founders who continued running their companies after taking them public were more likely to have the mental agility needed to reinvent their companies to take full advantage of ecommerce.

---

[2]Peter S. Cohan, "e-Profit: High Payoff Strategies for Capturing the Ecommerce Edge," (AMACOM: 2000).

[3]Clayton Christensen, "The Innovator's Dilemma: When New Technologies Cause Great Firms to Fail," (Harvard Business School Press, 1997).

When I wrote *Startup Cities*,[4] I realized that a region's most valuable business leaders were marathoners – who could turn an idea into a fast-growing public company. Marathoners – such as Amazon's Jeff Bezos or Facebook's Mark Zuckerberg – are likely to be far more open to investing in new growth opportunities than nonmarathoner CEOs. Thinking about this from the perspective of established store-based retailers raises a basic question: is it possible for a store-based retailer to hire in or develop a CEO who can compete with marathoners?

Since marathoners will eventually leave their companies, every company will need to answer this question. Simply put, over time it is inevitable that the challenges and opportunities facing a business will change. The question that a company's investors, customers, employees, partners, and communities must answer is whether the current CEO can overcome those challenges and capture the opportunities to keep the company growing profitably. The goal of this book is to help companies answer this question and – if the answer is no – to provide guidance on how they can hire a CEO with the mindset needed to achieve profitable growth.

How Can Strategic Mindset Help You Achieve Ecommerce Success?

Strategic mindset and the related corporate transformation levers we'll explore in this book can help you realize your ecommerce ambitions. The benefits of this framework will vary depending on where you sit. For example:

- **Bricks and mortar executives** will identify with one of the three strategic mindsets. The book will present case studies for each of these mindsets in six specific ecommerce market segments. The cases will help bricks and mortar executives to get an inside look at how other executives in their situation have tried to overcome the challenges and capture the opportunities of ecommerce. The case analyses will reveal key lessons from these case studies and suggest how they might take advantage of the lessons.
- **Bricks and mortar employees** will recognize which of the three strategic mindsets best characterizes the company. The case studies will help employees understand how a corporate transformation in their company could change what managers will expect them to do.

[4]Peter Cohan, "Startup Cities: Why Only a Few Cities Dominate the Global Startup Scene and What the Rest Should Do About It," (Apress: 2018).

Employees who welcome the challenge and learning associated with that change will find the book useful for preparing them by suggesting keys to success and pitfalls to avoid in their transformed roles. The book may help other employees realize that they will not be able to embrace the coming changes and may seek employment elsewhere.

- **Startup CEOs** could find the book valuable since it tips on its side the traditional narrative about startups disrupting big companies. Those founders will learn what to emulate and what to avoid by studying the mindsets and transformation of the bricks and mortar retailers presented in the book. They'll also benefit from the incumbent case studies – some of which could highlight new threats and opportunities that they had not previously considered. These insights might prompt them to adjust their growth strategies.
- **Business students:** The book will be particularly valuable to business students – those who want to start companies and those who work for large companies that are seeking to hold on to their customers by creating new strategic mindsets. The case studies, principles, and methodologies presented in the book will help students prepare to be more effective employees, managers, and executives.

Goliath Strikes Back Road Map

This book presents the findings of this research in two sections.

Part 1. Exploring Strategic Mindset by Industry

Chapter 1 introduces the core concepts of the book, while Chapters 2 through 7 examine more deeply how strategic mindset has played out in the way executives in seven different retail industries have grappled with the threats and opportunities of ecommerce: Consumer Electronics (Chapter 2), Video Entertainment (Chapter 3), Newspapers (Chapter 4), Furniture (Chapter 5), Groceries (Chapter 6), and Logistics (Chapter 7).

For each of these chapters, Part I covers the following topics:

- Analysis of the industry's structure, size, growth rate, and key growth and profitability drivers
- Strategic mindset maps of industry winners and losers
- Key implications for startup and incumbent CEOs
- Case studies of successful and unsuccessful startups and incumbents
- Key success and failure principles that emerge from the case studies
- Key assessment questions for industry startups and incumbents
- Key findings summary
- Conclusion

Part 2. Implications for Leaders

This second section of the book consists of its concluding chapter which summarizes the key insights from the preceding chapters to help incumbents change their strategic mindsets to capture the ecommerce edge. Chapter 8 helps leaders

- Identify whether their company faces a problem or opportunity gap
- Develop a competitive strategy to close the problem/opportunity gap
- Assess the quality of the vision and execution of the strategy
- Evaluate the fit between the CEO's strategic mindset and the company's future needs

If you want to change your mindset to win back customers from ecommerce upstarts, read on.

PART

I

Exploring Strategic Mindset by Industry

CHAPTER

1

Introduction

A CEO's strategic mindset is a set of beliefs about how the world works. Those beliefs come from different sources: including early role models such as parents, teachers, or bosses; education; and high-impact life experiences. A powerful example of CEO's strategic mindset is the case of Amazon founder and CEO, Jeff Bezos. Indeed, Bezos's influence on business has been so great that if he had chosen to become a physicist – which was his intention when he arrived at Princeton University – the industries which we'll explore in this book would likely look very different. Indeed, if you take away one thing from this book, understanding Bezos's strategic mindset – though you are unlikely to achieve anything near his level of success – will help make you more effective in whatever you do. Bezos's strategic mindset is based on five key elements:

- **Sustaining intellectual humility:** The most fundamental element of Bezos's strategic mindset is his realization that a leader should not assume that what worked for a company in the past will continue to work in the future. Unless a leader looks at every day with a fresh mind – what Bezos calls Day 1 – the company will begin to fail. As Bezos has been writing in his shareholder letters, "Day 2 is stasis. Followed by irrelevance. Followed by excruciating, painful decline. Followed by death. And that is why it is always Day 1." While a company might be able to harvest Day 2 for decades, he said, ultimately the result of that intellectual laziness is corporate death. The key to staying on Day 1 is to

P. S. Cohan, *Goliath Strikes Back*, https://doi.org/10.1007/978-1-4842-6519-2_1

maintain intellectual humility – asking the right questions, being honest about what you do not know, and investigating rigorously the answers to those unknowns to come up with fresh answers.

- **Obsessing over customers:** Bezos's Day 1 philosophy works because it puts a leader's primary focus on adapting the company to changing customer expectations – rather than being on the cutting edge of technology. The reason customer focus is so important is that he sees customers as a source of corporate vitality because they are "always beautifully, wonderfully dissatisfied…they always want something better." An essential process for a company with a Day 1 mindset is to keep trying new things. As he said, that means companies should "experiment patiently, accept failures, plant seeds, protect saplings, and double down when [they] see customer delight."
- **Fighting the filtering effect of bureaucracy:** As companies grow, they create formal processes which may have originally been created with the positive intention of increasing efficiency and minimizing mistakes. However, in most companies these processes take over key decisions – often causing the company to adapt less effectively to those delightfully dissatisfied customers. To fight the creeping power of processes such as market research surveys, Bezos urges product managers to do two things. First, they should spend so much time with customers that they develop strong intuition about how customers will respond to new ideas. As Bezos said, "A remarkable customer experience starts with heart, intuition, curiosity, play, guts, taste. You won't find any of it in a survey." Second, rather than justifying decisions by citing the process, product managers should observe outcomes and change the process to improve those outcomes.
- **Embracing external trends:** The way CEOs respond to strong trends outside the company is one of the clearest ways to identify their strategic mindset. A CEO who embraces external trends can harness them as growth tailwinds. Conversely, a CEO who ignores them will fight increasingly powerful headwinds – and probably not even know what is going wrong and what to do

about them. In 2016, Bezos saw machine learning as such a trend, and in light of the success of its autonomous Prime Air delivery drones; its Amazon Go convenience store that used machine vision to eliminate checkout lines; and Alexa, a cloud-based AI assistant, it is clear that Bezos embraces external trends.

- **Making high-quality decisions quickly:** Decisions are the primary product of senior leaders. If those leaders make well-informed decisions but take too long to reach those decisions and carry them out, they may fall behind rivals who make decisions and execute more quickly. A key element of Bezos's mindset is that leadership teams should make high-quality decisions quickly. He acknowledges that uncertainty can make it difficult to know whether a decision will yield the desired results and that the decision rules should vary depending on the nature of the decision. For example, a decision that can be quickly reversed if the outcome is bad should be made more quickly than a decision – such as spending billions of dollars to acquire a company – that will take much longer to undo if it's wrong. Bezos would rather decide with 70% of the information needed than delay to get 90%. In a nutshell, Bezos urges leaders to make decisions with less than optimal information because once the decision has been executed, the external reaction will either affirm the correctness of the decision or quickly help leaders identify and fix its flaws.[1]

This book focuses on the role of CEO strategic mindset in how bricks and mortar retailers respond to the threats and opportunities resulting from the growth of ecommerce. As my interviews with two experts on this topic reveal, the most successful retailers change their strategy and operations to deliver the best possible customer experience. While no bricks and mortar retailers took the threat of ecommerce seriously when Amazon got started, Nordstrom, Kohl's, and Target are among the most effective incumbent counter-attackers, and Harrods, Costco, TJX, and Ross Stores have been somewhat immune to the ravages of ecommerce, which have grown quite a bit since 1994 when Jeff Bezos quit his executive position at a New York hedge fund to drive to Seattle to start Amazon. Bezos saw that the Internet was growing at a 2,300% annual rate and realized it would eventually become a huge opportunity – starting with his focus on offering books online. In 2018, US ecommerce was a $517 billion industry growing at 15% annually (still a mere 14.3% of the $3.6 trillion retailing business) of which Amazon controlled a whopping 40%.[2]

What makes the difference between the bricks and mortar winners and losers? It is a simple concept that is hard to accomplish – give consumers a better buying experience. As Academic Director of Wharton's Baker Retailing Center, Thomas S. Robertson, explained in a September 2019 interview, the winners excel in four areas:

- **Omnichannel:** Since the customer uses both online and offline channels, successful retailers must integrate both seamlessly rather than thinking of them as competitive.
- **Customer experience:** Sephora is among the successful retailers that provide a "positive customer experience" through both technology and sales associate training.
- **Positioning:** Winning bricks and mortar retailers make clear choices about where they compete regarding "Who is their target market? Are they luxury or mass market? Are they competing on price or service?"
- **Innovation:** Ultimately companies that invest in store redesign and new ideas win out because "customers want novelty and new ideas" as "tired old stores are passing out of existence."[3]

While all this sounded obvious, inertia followed by the wrong response damaged many incumbents. As MIT Sloan School Senior Lecturer, Sharmila Chatterjee, explained in a September 2019 interview, "Bricks and mortar retailers thought ecommerce would be a component and adoption would be slower. They saw an adversarial relationship rather than realizing that a physical presence gave them a potential competitive advantage because going to stores was a social event for consumers. [Instead of building on this strength,] incumbents, such as Sears, responded with price discounts. [That was a bad strategy because] it constrained resources – limiting product selection, eliminating service, and producing long lines for returns which degraded the customer experience."[4]

The winners among the incumbent retailers follow Robertson's prescription of "superior omnichannel integration of online and bricks and mortar; creating a valuable in-store experience to which consumers are eager to return; educating sales associates who can take the customer's viewpoint (far better than a chat bot); and constantly innovating in acceptance of new technologies." Here are some that Robertson admired. As he said, "Sephora delivers a positive customer experience and does an excellent job of integrating digital and store with their app. Kohl's and Nordstrom have come under attack and are doing reasonably well. Both have been willing to take returns from others (Kohl's and Amazon) to increase store traffic. Kohl's has also shrunk a few of their stores by carving off space to lease to the German supermarket chain, Aldi. This reduces cost but also brings new customers to Kohl's. Nordstrom is innovative. It has created a portfolio of full-line department stores, Nordstrom Rack, Trunk Club, and a new concept, Nordstrom Local, that is essentially a 'service' location. Not all of this will work but the fight is admirable. Finally, I cannot ignore Walmart, which is doing very well in bricks and mortar and trying hard in online [though it is losing $1 billion in ecommerce] particularly with the purchase of Jet. They are having success with food ordering online and pickup at the store," he explained.[5]

Chatterjee was optimistic about Nordstrom and Target and concerned about Macy's. As she explained, "In Los Angeles, Nordstrom has two big stores with a small store between them. The concept is that you order online and pick up at the small store then consumers go to the large stores to browse. They are trying to tackle a big problem for the industry – the high cost of returning goods purchased online. Target is making some new changes that I have noticed. But Macy's has about 300 showcase stores that it is renovating and plans to use its other stores for self-service. I think consumers won't go to the self-service stores because of the poor customer experience which will initiate a doom loop." Some bricks and mortar stores were relatively immune from ecommerce. As Robertson pointed out, "The best defense is always a good offense and bricks and mortar retailers should build strategic walls before they lose customers. Some have; some have not. I would start with Harrods. They have done an admirable job of investing to beautify the store, training a knowledgeable set of associates, and partnering with major brands to essentially 'lease' space at Harrods. Costco has been reasonably immune to attack. TJX and Ross – the 'treasure hunt' stores – seem to have found protective cover."[6]

Figure 1-1. Three CEO Strategic Mindsets

This book explores three CEO strategic mindsets – depicted in Figure 1-1 – and how retailers use them to adapt to the challenges and opportunities of ecommerce:

- **Create the future:** This is the approach that Amazon's Jeff Bezos used – he repeatedly tried to invent new businesses which throw incumbents back on their heels.
- **Follow the leader:** Through different tactics such as acquiring Lore, putting its founder in charge of ecommerce, and allowing customers to order online and pick up at stores, this mindset is guiding Walmart's response to Amazon's incursions into many of its lines of business.
- **Head in the sand:** This mindset held back Bed Bath & Beyond from keeping up with upstarts with superior ecommerce and delivery services. Bed Bath & Beyond's founders believed that their success flowed from an obsession with minimizing costs – to wit, they banned Post-it notes and reluctantly spent the minimum amount to develop a bare-bones ecommerce capability. As a result, after 27 consecutive years of increased revenue, the company shrank in 2018 while losing $137 million in the fiscal year ending March 2019.[7]

Strategic mindset is more than just pointing at where the company should head – it also involves making key choices about five other corporate transformation levers which, if done correctly, enable a company to gain market share and grow faster. Figure 1-2 depicts how strategic mindset interacts with other levers that CEOs can pull to overcome the challenges and seize the opportunities of ecommerce.

Figure 1-2. Six Corporate Transformation Levers

While each CEO's strategic mindset is unique, the three CEO strategic mindsets lead to different ways of responding to the challenges and opportunities of ecommerce. Here is a general introduction to the other five corporate transformation levers:

- **Growth trajectory:** As I wrote in *Disciplined Growth Strategies*, companies seeking to sustain their growth must build growth trajectories. Leaders create growth trajectories by creating chains from five dimensions of growth (see Figure 1-3): customer group (current or new); product (built or acquired); geography (current or new); capabilities (current or new); and culture (current or new). Retailers that sustain their growth successfully excel at planning to jump on a new growth curve in a new dimension even as their current source of growth is peaking. By contrast, less successful retailers stick with the growth trajectories that worked in the past, despite evidence that their growth is slowing down.

- **Culture:** Culture is what a company's CEO and leadership team value most and how the company uses those values to select, motivate, reward, and punish people who work there. Retailers that successfully overcome the challenges and capture the opportunities of ecommerce reward employees who take responsibility for building and sustaining customer relationships as technology, customer needs, and the competitive landscape evolve. By contrast, less successful companies either have the wrong culture or fail to sustain the right one.
- **People:** When a retailer changes its growth trajectory or its culture, the CEO must assess whether the right people are in the company's key jobs. To do this well, the CEO must hire talented people who have succeeded in these roles before or promote current employees into these jobs. At the same time, leaders must part ways with people who can no longer contribute as effectively as others – which can be particularly painful for CEOs who must let go people with whom they have worked for years. Successful CEOs constantly monitor how well people are performing in their evolving roles and are actively engaged in recruiting and training key talent and letting go those who no longer fit, while less effective leaders resist the need to evaluate how well people are performing and are reluctant to replace longtime colleagues.
- **Operations:** To offer consumers a superior experience, retailers must adapt their operations. More specifically, successful retailers who offer consumers the opportunity to place orders online and pick them up at the store must deliver the items to the right store at the right time and hire and train customer service workers to help the customer pick up the items in the store. Less successful retailers fail to integrate their stores with online ordering, so when consumers arrive to pick up their orders, store personnel struggle to find the items in the store in a timely manner – or in some cases can't find the items at all.

- **Metrics:** When a CEO changes a company's operations, so must the means by which people are held accountable. More specifically, successful retailers seeking to provide customers with a better experience must collect specific data about their experience. Specific metrics to track customer experience trends might include the time it takes a customer to receive items ordered online once they arrive at the store, how many other items the customer purchases in the store after they retrieve the items they order online, how often the items they ordered online are not available when they arrive at the store, how satisfied customers say they are with the store experience, and how likely they are to recommend the store to others. The most successful retailers collect and analyze this data and reward managers and employees who are contributing to improvements in the customer experience.

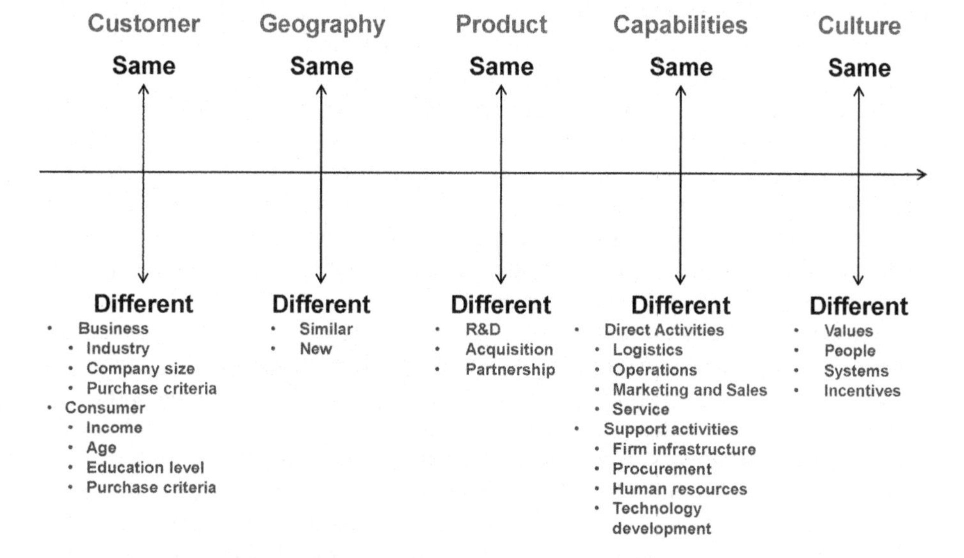

Figure 1-3. Five Dimensions of Growth

We will examine through case studies throughout the book how leaders deploy these corporate transformation levers differently depending on their strategic mindset.

Case Study: Target Stock Soars 91% As Outsider CEO Leads a Five-Year Customer Experience–Focused Transformation

Introduction

Bringing in a CEO with a different strategic mindset can lead to changes that turn a struggling retailer into one that consistently grows faster than investors expect as it delights customers with its product selection and ease of placing orders and taking delivery of those customer-pleasing products.

Case Scenario

That is what happened at Target. In 2014, Target was in trouble. So, it hired Brian Cornell, its first outside CEO. Over the next five years, his turnaround strategy – which featured an $8 billion investment announced in February 2017 – had nearly doubled its stock by mid-October 2019. Cornell took over in mid-August 2014. The peripatetic veteran of Michaels, Sam's Club, and PepsiCo grabbed the reins as Target was barely growing, struggling to recover from a massive consumer data breach and distracted by a disastrous expansion into Canada. Cornell was popular with investors due to his initial moves to jettison businesses that he thought did not fit with Target's corporate strategy. For example, he shuttered the Canadian operations and sold Target's $4 billion pharmacy business to CVS Health. As Charlie O'Shea, an analyst at Moody's, explained in an October 2019 interview, when it came to Canada, "Cornell ripped the band aid off. Canada should have been a great opportunity for Target but instead of expanding gradually after learning the local market which is what helped them succeed in the U.S., in Canada they opened too many stores at once. They wanted to prove to the world that they could do something different." But getting rid of failing businesses does nothing for a company's revenue growth. For that, a company needs to invest in growth opportunities. And Cornell created and sold Target's board on a package of store improvement and other initiatives that would require $7 billion in capital spending and $1 billion in operating expenses over three years. On February 28, 2017, Cornell announced this investment along with a terrible earnings report featuring below-forecast earnings for the final quarter of 2016 and a much worse than expected outlook for 2017.[8]

Investors reacted badly to Target's bold bet – sending its shares down 13% to around $58 as investors signaled their disapproval with its terrible results and outlook coupled with a big investment in stores when everyone knew that ecommerce was the future of retail. By the third quarter of 2019, Target had reported eight straight quarters of comparable sales increases…growing faster than rivals such as Macy's, Kohl's, and Walmart. How did Target fix itself? That $7 billion investment went to a blend of fundamental changes and a return to Target's roots. The fundamental *changes were offering what the industry describes as omnichannel – which means that consumers could shop, purchase, and take possession of goods any way they want. In 2017, Target acquired Grand Junction, a software-based solution for retailers, distributors, third-party logistics providers, and consumers. As Ben Gordon, whose firm Cambridge Capital invested in the company, explained in an October 2019 interview, "Grand Junction gave Target the opportunity to provide customers an alternative to Amazon Prime."*

And in December 2017, Target added to its omnichannel offerings by paying $550 million to acquire $99 subscription same-day delivery service Shipt – which by March 2019 was available in 1,500 stores. That month, consumers could order online and pick up at the curb in more than 1,000 stores – which saved Target 90% of the cost of fulfilling orders via warehouses.[9]

Analysts admired the results. As Tory Gundelach, VP of Retail Insights at Kantar Consulting, explained in an October 2019 interview, "Omnichannel means consumers can do business with Target through bricks and mortar, online, voice, and mobile [among others]. To do this effectively, Target's front-end technology personalizes a customer's experience so [she gets the] same message across all channels." This also requires changes in the so-called back end of the business. "Target has seven different fulfillment methods. [To execute well, Target] coordinates across the supply chain, logistics, fulfillment, and team members who pick and pack orders in the back of the store for curbside pickup and stack the store shelves." Another new element of Target's strategy was its 100 small stores in urban locations – these stores gave Target access to customers in places where Walmart did not operate. The small stores generated nearly $900 in annual sales per square foot – about three times the figure for a typical suburban store.

The return to Target's roots manifested itself across the board. Target articulated its mission – "to help all families discover the joy in everyday life" – which inspired and empowered more of its 320,000 workers.[10]

In addition to changing its culture and operations, Target refreshed its stores by getting rid of linoleum floors and displaying clothing on mannequins (it expected to do that for 1,000 of its 1,800 stores by the end of 2020) and improved how it displays items to shoppers. The company also brought back "Tarzhay" – its blend of private label, such as its high margin $2 billion revenue children's line Cat & Jack – and only-at-Target exclusives made by other companies. Collectively accounting for about 30% of sales, Tarzhay "gives shoppers a reason to come into its stores," noted Gundelach. Those shoppers tended to be younger and wealthier than those at Walmart. In 2019, the average Target shopper was 42.5 years old and sported a household income of $77,610. That was 3.5 years younger and $13,408 richer than the average Walmart shopper.[11]

Could Target keep growing? In 2019, a Wall Street analyst estimated Target had a $9 billion opportunity to win customers from retailers that had been cutting back stores and filing for bankruptcy. Target added customers from bankrupt rivals like

Gymboree, the Sports Authority, and Toys "R" Us. And in 2016, when Victoria's Secret stopped selling most of its women's swimwear, Target took nine months to launch its own women's bathing suits – and by October 2019 led the United States there. Ultimately Target's ability to sustain its growth depended on how quickly it could identify and capture new opportunities. To do that, Target had the advantage of taking its cue from customers and being "data driven" rather than imposing its vision from the top-down as JC Penney did, explained Sucharita Kodali, Forrester Research Vice President and Principal Analyst, in an October 2019 interview. Target – which received a Glassdoor rating of 3.4/5 from 34,000 reviews in that month – had room to enhance employee engagement. Despite paying workers higher wages, some of them "say the chain has cut their shifts, costing them pay, endangering their eligibility for the company's health insurance coverage and making it generally more difficult to do their jobs properly," according to RetailWire, which noted that Target had "pledged to raise its minimum wage to $15 an hour" by the end of 2020. Target also has room for improvement when it comes to produce. But in 2019 Target was doing something about it – rolling out a new private grocery brand, Good & Gather, that would feature more than 2,000 items without artificial flavors and sweeteners. In October 2019, a Target spokesperson said that Food and Beverage was "a big reason our guests like shopping and we've been seeing consistent growth and market share gains in Food and Beverage for well over a year."[12]

Case Analysis

Target's turnaround illustrates the effectiveness of the six corporate transformation levers in the hands of a CEO with a *Follow the Leader* strategic mindset. Simply put, Cornell enabled Target to catch up with many of the best aspects of Amazon's ecommerce strategy while offering some improvements of its own. Cornell articulated a compelling mission; he refreshed Target's growth trajectory by offering compelling products, improving the look of its stores, replacing many of its top executives and boosting worker pay, redesigning its operations (with the help of Target's chief operating officer), and most likely changing the way it holds its people accountable.

Strategic Mindset Research

To investigate these questions and refine my strategic mindset model, I interviewed professors and industry experts. I researched the performance and prospects of six industries and wrote in-depth case studies of how CEOs who embodied the three strategic mindsets tried to capture the opportunities and fend off the threats in these industries. More specifically, I investigated how the CEO's mindsets developed during their careers, how those strategic mindsets shaped their strategic choices, and how these choices affected their company's financial performance and prospects. Finally, I analyzed the case studies and highlighted the implications of these cases for different groups of readers.

Read on to explore how CEO strategic mindset shaped six industries – beginning with consumer electronics.

CHAPTER

2

Consumer Electronics

In a large industry that is slowly getting smaller, leaders of incumbent firms can defy the moribund industry by taking market share away from less nimble rivals. An important way to do that is to understand the broad trends driving the change in the industry and tack the company so that those powerful winds are pushing the company forward rather than holding it back. This comes to mind in considering the consumer electronics industry in which consumers purchased electronics through retail stores and online. Lessons for leaders include

- **Build on your strengths:** In the consumer electronics industry, the largest retail store chains enjoyed the advantage of being within driving distance of a large proportion of the consuming public. Despite the advent of ecommerce, consumers generally did not want to purchase a new consumer electronics product unless they had tried it out in a showroom and asked questions of knowledgeable salespeople. Compared to online-only rivals, such incumbents offered consumers a better experience when it came to shopping for a new electronics product.

P. S. Cohan, *Goliath Strikes Back*, https://doi.org/10.1007/978-1-4842-6519-2_2

- **Partner to bolster your weaknesses:** Sadly, there was a flip side to a store-based retailer's advantage in the electronics shopping process. Once a consumer had decided which specific product to purchase, the advantage shifted to online-only vendors. That is because the Internet enabled consumers to search for the least expensive way to purchase and take delivery of the product they wanted to buy. To overcome this weakness, store-based retailers adapted: they sold the product to consumers at the lowest price available online, they enabled consumers to take delivery more quickly than online-only vendors in the store, and they even opened up showrooms for their online rivals to display their own products.
- **Create happy employees and customers:** If employees are engaged with a company's mission and values, they are more likely to be more creative and work more intensely to serve customers well so they will advocate enthusiastically on the company's behalf to people they know and continue to purchase there over time. Incumbent consumer electronics retailers may have a legacy of creating happy employees and customers. However, it takes a CEO with the right mindset to reignite this powerful motivating force.
- **Choose your successor wisely:** Leaders who build successful companies must choose successors with a *Create the Future* or *Follow the Leader* mindset. As we will see in the following Best Buy case, when the company's board appointed a CEO with a *Follow the Leader* mindset to replace an abruptly jettisoned *Head in the Sand* CEO. That proved to be a wise choice as the successor implemented many of the changes in strategy and culture highlighted earlier – and the company's stock roughly tripled as a result.

These implications emerge from examining the large consumer electronics industry that was slowly getting smaller. Despite the growth in consumer spending, by November 2019, IBISWorld expected industry revenues to end the five-year period through 2019 down at an annualized 2.2% rate to $85.7 billion – a considerable drop from its 2000 peak level of $112.5 billion. Moreover, by 2024, the consumer electronics retailing industry was expected to be slightly smaller.[1]

A big reason for the industry's revenue decline was the price-cutting that helped propel online consumer electronics retailing at a much faster 11% annual rate. Consumers also shifted their purchases from stores to online suppliers like Amazon due to their greater convenience and wider product variety. Online retailers operated with lower overhead costs than traditional bricks and mortar stores and passed their cost savings to consumers by offering lower prices. Store-based consumer electronics retailers reduced their prices to remain competitive, shuttered unprofitable operations, and laid off employees to boost margins. By the end of 2019, consumer electronics industry employment had declined at a 2.3% annual rate to 329,256 workers during which time the number of store locations had fallen at an annualized 3.2% to 51,615. However, the cost cutting was insufficient to keep industry profitability from declining. Indeed, earnings before interest and taxes as a percent of revenue fell from 4.6% in 2014 to 4.1% in 2019. As a larger proportion of consumers abandon store-based retailers, overall, industry revenue was forecast to decline an annualized 0.2% to $84.8 billion between 2019 and 2024.[2]

Product innovation was the most powerful force brightening the gloomy consumer electronics retailing picture. While innovation in formerly growth-propelling product categories such as TVs and personal computers had stagnated, the popularity of new tablets and smartphones in the five years ending 2019 helped to spur demand growth. However, that growth attracted competitors who provided better products at lower prices with longer useful lives – thus accelerating the maturation of these product categories. Moreover, online streaming of video and music dampened demand for CDs and DVDs.[3] By 2019, the industry appeared to lack consumer electronics product innovations that would counter the slowing industry growth expected as these established product categories continued to mature and decline.[4]

Store-based consumer electronics retailers – most notably Best Buy (which we will examine in greater depth later in this chapter) – were changing their business strategies to compete more effectively. To win over new customers and keep current ones, such retailers did the following:

- Sited stores in well-populated, easy-to-access locations with high foot traffic
- Controlled stock in stores to satisfy demand and limit excess inventory buildup
- Hired, trained, and motivated a skilled workforce that excelled at customer service
- Displayed products in a clear and appealing manner
- Partnered effectively with the most popular consumer electronics brands

- Provided excellent customer service by conveying a clear understanding of product benefits and features and offering extended warranties and report services
- Supplied sophisticated custom installation of home entertainment products[5]

Covid-19 made the anticipated decline in industry revenues much worse – yet well-positioned companies such as Best Buy found a way to benefit. By July 2020, Covid-19 was expected to reduce industry revenue by 10% in 2020 due to the economic slowdown and temporary store closures. Demand for consumer electronics was expected to be limited by lower per capital disposable income and lower consumer spending. Consumer electronics retailers that could not absorb the costs and lack of revenue were expected to cut employees or exit the industry. Best Buy appeared to be one of the survivors.[6] While it suffered a roughly 30% decline in revenue as consumers stayed at home and away from stores, Best Buy furloughed employees to lower its operating costs. By May 2020, Best Buy's ability to take orders online and pick them up at the store positioned the company well for a surprising increase in orders as telecommuting consumers purchased more electronics online. One analyst, Telsey Advisory Group, saw Best Buy gaining market share and benefiting from that boost in demand. Another analyst concluded that Best Buy's technology focus and growing services business would enable the company to gain more market share thanks to its strong in-store and online execution and innovative products that appealed to its customers.[7] By July 2020, Best Buy stock reached an all-time high thanks to higher than expected revenue. Since reopening its stores in mid-June, Best Buy sales had risen 15%, and it promised permanent wage increases for employees. Online sales soared 255%, thanks to purchases of computers, tablets, and appliances, and online sales remained 185% higher after stores reopened.[8]

Strategic Mindsets of Consumer Electronics Industry Winners and Losers

Gaining market share in this declining industry required leaders to envision and execute an effective competitive strategy to provide an industry-leading consumer experience. Whether a strategy yielded market share gains or losses depended to a large extent on which of the three strategic mindsets we introduced in Chapter 1 – *Create the Future*, *Follow the Leader*, and *Head in the Sand* – the CEO adopted. Here are some general observations based on the collision of these three mindsets with consumer electronics industry reality explored in the following case studies:

- **Leaders with *Create the Future* and *Follow the Leader* mindsets are winners:**
    - *Create the Future* works well if leaders are intellectually humble in pursuit of delivering consumer ever more value – for example, benefits for the money – than rivals do. Rather than imposing conclusions on underlings, intellectual humility drives the leader to seek information from employees, customers, partners, and technology and industry experts. This mindset leads to new products and better execution that yield industry-beating revenue growth and – if that growth continues to exceed investors' expectations – boost the company's stock price.
    - *Follow the Leader* is a mindset of CEOs who – as we saw in the Target case in Chapter 1 – successfully turn around a company following a downturn. Such a leader boosts employee satisfaction – which inspires employees to provide customers with new products and better service. At the same time, the leader partners to supply new products that customers are eager to buy, redesigns operations to reduce cost and speed up customer order fulfillment, and upgrades systems and training to deliver excellent after-sales service. While these changes may initially require a large investment, over time they can reward shareholders through faster-than-expected growth and profitability.
- ***Head in the Sand* leaders preside over failure:** Some CEOs brought in to turn around troubled consumer electronics retailers fail. Often founders can make the company quite successful; however, they fumble in choosing their successors. While the founder's mental model might hinge on creating the best environment for employees to provide better value to customers, the successor might focus too heavily on meeting quarterly financial metrics. Such a CEO may ignore rapidly growing rivals, new technologies, and changing customer needs. And such a *Head in the Sand* mindset might lead the CEO to cut thousands of employees and buy back stock. Abrupt, mass layoffs can discourage employees who remain and result in poor product selection and service. Customers will then flee to faster-growing rivals – causing

revenues to plunge. Ultimately the company could be stuck with inventory that customers will not buy and could lack the cash needed to buy new merchandise that customers prefer.

Consumer Electronics Industry Startup and Incumbent Success and Failure Case Studies

These general observations play out in the following case studies. Amazon's *Create the Future* mindset enabled it to surpass Best Buy as the leading consumer electronics retailer. Best Buy's *Follow the Leader* mindset drove its CEO to shrink to a profitable core and grow at expectation-beating rates by inspiring its employees, ending showrooming, and partnering with suppliers such as Amazon. A *Head in the Sand* mindset contributed to Circuit City's fatal self-inflicted wound which resulted in its November 2008 bankruptcy filing – and, three months later, the liquidation of its assets.

Success: Amazon Takes the Top Spot in Consumer Electronics Retailing

Introduction

Creating the future can accelerate a company's growth rate into the fast lane if it makes customers more eager to buy from that company than from its peers. Amazon did this – propelling its consumer electronics revenue up at more than twice the rate of its leading competitor. As a result, in 2017 Amazon took the top spot in the consumer electronics retailing industry from Best Buy.

Case Scenario

In April 2018, Amazon took away the top spot from Best Buy on Dealerscope's Top 101 Consumer Electronics Retailers list of annual retail consumer electronics sales. Amazon's 2017 consumer electronics revenue grew 18.5% to over $5.3 billion – surpassing the 8.5% growth rate of Best Buy – which had topped the list since it was launched in 2013.[9] Amazon extended its lead in 2018, enjoying a 21% growth in its consumer electronics revenues to $41.26 billion – almost $7 billion more than the number two Best Buy.[10] Amazon's move into the top position was no surprise to Deutsche Bank which in 2016 noted that Amazon accounted for 90% of the $5.6 billion growth in consumer electronics sales posted nationwide in 2015. Though Amazon had a mere 6.2% share and ranked fourth on the list of top 100 US *electronics retailers, its consumer electronics sales grew 28% in 2015 way faster than Best Buy's 3.8% that year. So Deutsche Bank was then confident that Amazon would eventually take the lead in US consumer electronics retailing.*[11]

Two forces drove Amazon's rapid growth: its successful design, manufacturing, and delivery of new consumer electronics products and its ability to offset its weakness as a place for consumers to browse or discover consumer electronics, with an industry-leading ability to offer consumers a wide product selection, competitive prices, timely delivery, and excellent after-sales service.[12] *Amazon launched its first website in 1995, but an important turning point in its move to dominate consumer electronics was its 2007 launch of the Kindle ebook reader. While Amazon priced the first black-and-white version of the Kindle below $400, the product evolved into a personal tablet. However, by November 2019, Kindle sales were rapidly declining as more people used their smartphones or tablets to read books or listened to audiobooks on these devices.*[13] *Fortunately, Amazon's consumer electronics product line included other devices such as its Echo smart speakers and its Alexa voice assistant which RBC Capital Markets Analyst Mark Mahaney estimated could generate between $18 billion and $19 billion in total sales by 2021. Amazon's Alexa revenue would derive from three sources, according to Mahaney, low-margin device sales of $9.2 billion; additional ecommerce revenue resulting from sales via Alexa, and Alexa Skills revenue – 30% of whose $2 billion in revenue went to Amazon*[14] *– delivered via over 100 million Alexa-enabled devices.*[15]

An overarching force driving Amazon's market share wins was its ability to outperform rivals in meeting customer purchase criteria which included detailed product descriptions; clear product images; useful customer product reviews; accurate product information; easy online ordering, delivery, and returns (if needed); and excellent after-sales service. Amazon excelled at operating warehouses which ordered and received from suppliers and stored inventory on shelves. When consumers placed an order, workers in the fulfillment centers picked, packed, shipped, and provided customer service for the products. With Amazon's Prime Service, consumers could receive delivery within two days (approaching one day).[16]

Case Analysis

More than any competitor in the consumer electronics retailing industry, Amazon's mindset was tuned to creating the future. Bezos's Day I philosophy – which kept the company in a constant race to reinvent itself to keep delighting its demand customers – pushed the company to create and execute market share–winning strategies. In consumer electronics, Amazon benefited from its invention of new products – including the Kindle and the Alexa product family including its Echo smart speakers. While these new products contributed to Amazon's rapid revenue growth rate, its process for online ordering and fulfillment provided an excellent customer experience.

Success: Stock Soars 330% As Outside CEO Creates Meaning for Best Buy Workers and Consumers

Introduction

While Amazon's rapid growth represented a challenge to all its rivals, it also presented an opportunity to a store-based retailer whose CEO had the right strategic mindset. In the consumer electronics retailing industry – as in any industry that sells directly to a consumer – that mindset was based on a specific mental model of business success: higher returns to shareholders were a by-product of attracting and motivating talented employees who strove to provide consumers more benefits for the price than did rivals, as I described in *Value Leadership*.[17] While that mental model was a critical starting point, to boost a store-based retailer's financial results, in parallel the CEO changed the company's strategy, operations, and systems for holding people accountable.

Case Scenario

Hubert Joly inherited a mess at Best Buy. For years, the dominant narrative in tech had been about startups disrupting established companies and large companies' flat-footed responses to the challenge. In August 2012, Joly, who had previously run hospitality company Carlson, took over as Best Buy's CEO following a whopping $1.7 billion loss and the departure of its previous CEO in the wake of a "close relationship" with a female employee, according to Bloomberg. By the time Joly handed over Best Buy's reins to Corie Barry, who had recently served as its chief financial and strategic transformation officer, in June 2019, its shares had soared 330% from $20 to about $68, and in the quarter ending May 2019, the 125,000-employee electronics retailer had earned a 3% net profit margin.[18]

There are many things Joly did to turn around Best Buy – but the most powerful, surprising, and universally applicable thing he did was to change the company's approach to managing its people. Instead of treating Best Buy employees as costs to be minimized – his predecessor eliminated employee discounts – Joly prioritized creating meaning for them. More specifically, one of Joly's early changes at Best Buy was to describe the company's purpose and to encourage Best Buy's managers to listen to employees' dreams and help connect their dreams with Best Buy's purpose. This was a powerful and controversial idea. As Joly said in November 2018, "[Making money is a company's] imperative ... But it is not the purpose. I believe the purpose of a company is to contribute to the common good: its customers, its employees, and the community in which it operates. If you can connect the search for meaning of the individual with the purpose of the company, then magical things happen." Best Buy applied the idea of Value Leadership in an interesting way: encouraging managers in its stores to connect each employee's search for meaning with the company's purpose. This worked well in a Best Buy store near Boston. As Joly said in a July 2019 meeting with students at his alma mater, the French business school HEC, "I watched the head of [this store] ask his employees what their dreams were. One said he wanted to buy a house for his family. The manager told him that they would work together to help him develop his skills, move up in the company, and make his dream a reality. Achieving something significant does not have to involve huge humanitarian efforts. My personal goal is to make a positive difference for the people around me. It is basically a very limited goal! But it's the meaning of my life."[19]

Joly not only shed unproductive people and operations, he encouraged more customers to visit and purchase from Best Buy, by changing its strategic posture toward its customers, its employees, and Amazon. He also pruned noncore operations. To that end, Best Buy first sought to eliminate costs by making its processes more efficient. He estimated that 80% of Best Buy's $2 billion in costs were nonsalary expenses. For example, to that end, Best Buy saved $200 million by working with suppliers to design and ship TVs in a way that would keep them from breaking before they arrived at a customer's house.[20] But Best Buy also cut about 2,000 middle managers in early 2014; selectively closed some 50 stores between 2014 and 2018; exited a European retail joint venture in 2013; sold off its stores in China in 2014; and in 2018 killed its Best Buy mobile business, closing the remaining 257 small stand-alone stores. What is more? Joly began his Best Buy tenure by spending a week with associates in a St. Cloud, Minn. Store. They told him about a devastating practice called showrooming – customers who visited the store, talked to Best Buy employees but bought from an online purveyor like Amazon. Best Buy put the kibosh on showrooming by announcing that it would match online prices. Associate feedback persuaded Joly to invest in a faster, easy-to-search website and to restore the employee discounts that his predecessor had eliminated.[21] These moves helped Best Buy to reduce worker turnover from 50% to 30%.[22] Best Buy also introduced a store pickup system – enabling consumers to order online and pick up in the store within an hour with help from its convenient locations (70% of the US population lived within 15 minutes of a Best Buy store).[23] And Joly clearly articulated the role of store associates: to be trusted advisors who help customers evaluate and choose new technology. In April 2018, Best Buy inked a deal with Amazon to retail exclusively its Fire TV Edition smart TVs. Joly concluded that the benefits to Best Buy – including Amazon's investment in the Best Buy stores and the popularity of its product with customers – outweighed the costs of helping its rival. Best Buy also derives similar benefits from its partnerships with Apple, Microsoft, Samsung, Google, LG, Canon, Nikon, AT&T, Sprint, and Verizon.[24]

Joly's strategic mindset was a powerful force for enabling Best Buy's turnaround. In a Stanford Business School class, The Industrialist's Dilemma, which featured Joly, Management Lecturer Maxwell Wessel highlighted three key elements:

- **See the headwinds as the tailwinds:** *Joly took over at Best Buy in the face of what most observers saw as challenges. Categories were decaying rapidly while new consumer electronics and categories were emerging just as quickly. Ecommerce vendors were taking share of many of the high volume, small box goods that Best Buy distributed. But he was able to see these challenges as opportunities. Some of the new categories were connected devices. And Joly saw an opportunity to provide customers with the ability to make individual products operate together seamlessly. Joly's change in mindset enabled Best Buy to "reorient, reinvest, and get behind a changing strategy."*
- **Be a systems integrator for the consumer:** *A related mindset change was Joly's orientation toward consumer electronics makers. Since Best Buy made its own private label products, he felt drawn toward viewing other product vendors as rivals. However, Joly resisted that urge and transformed Best Buy could into a systems integrator acting on behalf of its customers. Joly hired, trained, and motivated store associates who could assemble the best collection of components for each customer experience and make the components work together.*
- **Treat the supplier like a customer:** *Joly's focus on creating value for customers made it easier for him to see how suppliers – even those that competed directly with Best Buy such as Amazon – were making products that customers wanted to buy. Therefore, Best Buy helped suppliers to "make their store footprint as desirable as possible and helped them build a distribution strategy around Best Buy." To that end, Best Buy became a critical link in its supplier's product design – helping to set product standards – and working with suppliers to orchestrate product launches. Best Buy "was building a thoughtful strategy — a complementary set of activities — to differentiate their position in an ever-fragmenting world of products," concluded Wessel.*[25]

Case Analysis

The CEO's strategic mindset can either help or hurt a company's performance. In Best Buy's case, what was most important to the turnaround under Joly was his approach to thinking about the consumer electronics business. In his view, business success flowed from inspiring and developing talented employees who would build integrated home entertainment systems to satisfy customers' unique requirements. Bearing this in mind, Joly cut people and operations that distracted the company from his vision, trained and empowered Best Buy's store associates, curtailed showrooming by matching online prices, fixed its systems and logistics to enable customers to order online and pick up at its stores, and partnered with suppliers of popular brands – including its rival, Amazon. The lesson is clear: the right mindset coupled with a compelling strategy and excellent execution can enable a follower to improve its performance.

Failure: Circuit City Files for Bankruptcy After Ignoring Industry Changes

Introduction

Success can sow the seeds of failure. That is because in too many successful companies leaders surround themselves with sycophantic executives and rubber-stamp boards of directors who embrace every idea the CEO proposes. A critical corollary to this rule of operation is that employees and managers who report to those executives know that if they supply information that challenges the way things are being done, they will soon find themselves sidelined or out of a job. This confirmation bias – an executive's urge to receive information that reinforces their prior beliefs, and ignore the rest – presents an excellent business opportunity for a rival focused on delivering the best value to customers. If your most significant competitor refuses to keep up with changes in its industry, that rival's customers are up for grabs, and you would be remiss not to take advantage of the opportunity.

Case Scenario

This comes to mind in considering the November 10, 2008, bankruptcy of Circuit City. At the time, the Richmond, Va. company was the second largest consumer electronics retailer behind Best Buy. In the fiscal year ending February 2008, it operated over 700 stores, employed more than 48,000 "associates," and reported annual sales of $11.7 billion and a $321 million net loss.[26] *In the week prior to its bankruptcy filing, Circuit City announced plans to close 155 stores and cut 17% of its workforce. And its bankruptcy filing left in the lurch suppliers such as HP, which was owed $118.8 million, Samsung (a $115.9 million creditor), and Sony ($60 million) – who topped the list of its 100,000 creditors.*[27]

Circuit City was founded as a television store by Samuel Wurtzel in 1949. The company enjoyed tremendous success in the 1980s and 1990s but stopped adapting to the changing competitive environment after that, according to David Schick at Stifel Nicolaus. Its complacency became most pronounced in the late 1990s. Circuit City chose inconvenient store locations, and consumers opted to shop at the more convenient Walmart stores; it was slow to supply its customers gaming technology *and failed to promote products from popular vendors like Apple; and its website was underdeveloped just as Amazon was beginning to surge in popularity. Best Buy was nimbler in all these areas, and by the third quarter of 2008, Circuit City – which could not persuade customers to purchase the electronics in its inventory – posted a $239 million loss. For the same quarter, Best Buy increased its sales and earned a $200 million profit.*[28] *Circuit City further endangered its survival by swapping cash for a $1 billion stock buyback program between 2003 and 2007. Four months after filing for Chapter 11, Circuit City was liquidated after it failed to restructure its finances or find a buyer who would keep it operating.*[29]

While Circuit City made other management missteps, the most significant one was its early 2007 decision to reduce costs by firing 3,400 experienced and highly paid workers, including salespeople, and replacing them with 2,100 lower-paid hourly workers. That same year, then-CEO Philip Schoonover received about $7 million in compensation. Customers reacted angrily to replacing Circuit City's experienced salespeople – causing hundreds of thousands of entries in response to a search on Circuit City customer complaints.[30] *It is surprising that Schoonover – who from 1995 to 2004 was a Best Buy executive, and most recently its EVP of Customer Centricity,*[31] *before taking over as Circuit City CEO in 2006 – did not realize that replacing experienced people with lower-paid novices would damage Circuit City's reputation with customers. Schoonover's boneheaded blunder was a fatal self-inflicted wound that sent customers to the competition – leaving Circuit City with piles of unsold inventory. As a result, it could not buy fresh products or pay off its debts. The founder's son Alan Wurtzel – who was Circuit City's CEO from 1972 to 1986, its board chairman from 1986 to 1994, and its vice chairman from 1994 to 2001 – suggested in 2012 that Circuit City did not adapt to changing consumer tastes or buying patterns. Wurtzel said that his successors "dismissed Best Buy as a marginally profitable company that wouldn't survive." Wurtzel's immediate successor Rick Sharp, CEO from 1986 to 2000, was no slouch – during his tenure, revenue increased from $1 billion to $12.6 billion, and profit surged from $22 million to $327 million. But Sharp was more interested in new ventures such as CarMax, a discount car rental company that was spun out in 2002, than in Circuit City's core electronics retailing business.*[32] *Of Schoonover, Wurtzel concluded, "He may have understood merchandise, but he didn't understand a damn thing about the Circuit City culture. The way he hired and fired and demeaned people. … So, the culture that my dad had built, that I had nurtured, that Rick had perpetuated, was destroyed."*[33]

Case Analysis

Circuit City suffered from a succession of CEOs who ignored changing customer needs, new technology, and the threat from upstart rivals such as Best Buy and Amazon. During Sharp's tenure, Circuit City invested capital and management attention in new businesses that distracted from its core. And rivals took advantage of the opportunity to offer customers a better value proposition – including more convenient locations and a better merchandise selection. The final coup de grâce for Circuit City was inflicted by its last CEO, Schoonover, who saw salespeople as expenses to be cut rather than builders and keepers of long-term customer relationships.

Consumer Electronics Industry Case Study Takeaways

The takeaways from these case studies have varying implications depending on where you sit.

Bricks and Mortar Executives

- **Do:** Based on the Amazon and Best Buy cases, bricks and mortar executives may create competitive advantage by
    - Inspiring their employees to work with customers to help them make the right purchases for their needs – rather than trying to push their own products.
    - Identifying popular products, such as those from Amazon, that their customers want to learn about in a store before purchasing. Executives should explore a partnership with such brands as described in the Best Buy case study.
    - Regularly refreshing their merchandising mix to add products that consumers want to buy and eliminate unpopular items that sit in inventory.
    - Using knowledge of their customer's buying behavior and unmet needs to develop proprietary new products.
    - Adapting their systems and logistics networks so customers can order online and pick up at the store on the same day.
- **Do not:** Based on the Circuit City case, bricks and mortar executives should avoid its self-destructive tactics during a business downturn such as
    - Projecting credibility-defying levels of optimism to investors about an imminent financial turnaround.
    - Diversifying into new industries rather than adapting the core business to changing customer needs, upstart rivals, and new technologies

- Dismissing the significance of fast-growing rivals rather than investigating the reasons for their growth
- Viewing employees as expenses to be cut rather than sources of excellent service that help the company to attract and keep customers
- Buying back stock to boost earnings per share rather than investing in new merchandise that customers want to buy and improvements in the company's systems and logistics networks

Bricks and Mortar Employees

- **Do:** Based on the Amazon and Best Buy cases, bricks and mortar employees may seek to shape their workplaces by
  - Becoming expert advisors to customers seeking to match product benefits to their unique needs
  - Working with their managers to align their dreams with the company's purpose
- **Do not:** Based on the Circuit City case, bricks and mortar employees should consider seeking employment elsewhere if the company's CEO
  - Focuses exclusively on satisfying Wall Street's quarterly earnings expectations.
  - Avoids spending time in stores with employees and customers
  - Cuts spending on product development
  - Views employees as costs to be reduced

Startup CEOs

- **Do:** Based on the Amazon and Best Buy cases, Startup CEOs may scale their companies by
  - Creating a compelling mission that attracts and inspires talented people to create more value for customers than rivals do.
  - Investing in growth opportunities which their superior skills enable them to capture more effectively than Best Buy and/or Amazon can. Ultimately such investments could increase in value as these larger companies employ the startup's service or acquire the startup after it grows.

- **Do not:** Based on the Circuit City case, Startup CEOs should avoid its self-destructive tactics during a business downturn such as
    - Partnering with large companies that are overly focused on quarterly investor expectations and lack concern for employee and customer satisfaction.
    - Overspending on perks that do not add value to customers – which in a downturn must be slashed quickly
    - Underinvesting in new product development and more efficient business processes

Business Students

- **Do:** Based on the Amazon and Best Buy cases, business students may seek employment with companies that
    - Inspire their employees to work with customers to help them make the right purchases for their needs – rather than trying to push their own products
    - Articulate the right values – seeking to inspire talented people to create value for customers – and act accordingly
    - Invest in training and developing talented people so they can take on more responsibility
    - Encourage employees to brainstorm and recommend innovations that can benefit the company and its customers
- **Do not:** Based on the Circuit City case, business students should avoid companies that
    - Focus exclusively on meeting quarterly financial targets
    - Lack clearly articulated values and/or act in ways that undermine those values
    - Give lip services to valuing employees but ignore their ideas and fail to invest in training and developing them
    - Starve product development and customer service to hold costs down
    - Buy back stock to boost earnings per share

Do You Have the Strategic Mindset of a Consumer Electronics Industry Winner?

If you answer in the affirmative to these questions, you have a winning strategic mindset. If not, you must decide whether to change your mindset, strategy, and execution or find a job that better suits your strengths and interests:

- Do you know what dissatisfies your customers about buying from your company?
- Are you improving products and processes to replace that customer dissatisfaction with delight?
- Does your company have a compelling mission that attracts talented people?
- Are your managers helping your people align their dreams with your company's mission?
- Are you cutting costs that do not add value to customers and investing the savings in happier employees and a better customer experience?

Conclusion

The consumer electronics industry is getting smaller and less profitable. While some large companies have suffered the consequences of burying their head in the sand, others are gaining market share by creating the future and by following the leader effectively. While those winners build from their strengths and bolster their weaknesses to offer customers the merchandise they demand and ever-improving service, the losers ignore fast-growing rivals and starve investment in employees and innovation in a bid to satisfy investors' quarterly profit expectations. The successes and failures of consumer electronics rivals reveal the powerful interactions between a leader's mindset and the strategies and operational decisions that foreshadow their financial success or failure. In Chapter 3, we will examine how these interactions play out in the video entertainment industry.

CHAPTER

3

Video Entertainment

Video entertainment was delivered to consumers via three different technologies. Satellite and cable broadcasters were declining rapidly while so-called over-the-top (OTT) content providers – which did not require consumers to pay cable or satellite broadcasting fees – were booming. Satellite and cable broadcasters were shrinking because compared to OTT content providers, their prices were too high and the quality and variety of their content were relatively poor. Satellite and cable TV providers could compete with OTT service providers by trying to offer their own high-quality content. Yet their profit models were dependent on consumers paying satellite and cable fees and advertisers "polluting" the content consumers were viewing. Meanwhile OTT service providers were in a constant battle to spend on new content that would enable them to increase the number of subscribers each month. The video entertainment industry's dynamism offered excellent examples of how important a CEO's strategic mindset is to achieve long-term success. Lessons for leaders include

- **Evaluate your strategy through the eyes of customers:** Since leaders are surrounded by members of their executive team, it is natural for them to view their company from the inside out. In all industries, leaders with this perspective are at a competitive disadvantage because they are more likely to evaluate

P. S. Cohan, *Goliath Strikes Back*, https://doi.org/10.1007/978-1-4842-6519-2_3

options for the future from the perspective of how much they will increase the value of the company's largest lines of business. That perspective could work well if those business lines are all leaders in rapidly growing markets. However, if the markets from which the company derives its revenue are stagnating or shrinking, this inside-out perspective could result in decisions that position the company poorly for the future. To avoid this problem, leaders must identify, listen to, and target their video entertainment business strategies to customer groups that represent the most significant future growth opportunities for the company.

- **Resist the urge to defend old business strategies:** Viewing a company from the outside in can be particularly painful for leaders of companies that offer a weaker selection of over-priced video entertainment content. Such companies will try to preserve this competitively inferior customer positioning because they will see the alternative – offering an industry-leading collection of content at a lower price – as producing weaker financial results. In the long run, defending an outmoded and uncompetitive business strategy could endanger the company's long-term survival.
- **Choose your successor wisely:** Leaders of legacy video entertainment companies – for example, those that broadcast via satellite or cable – who cannot abandon their increasingly uncompetitive business strategies should appoint successors who can. Such successors are likely to be CEOs with *Create the Future* or *Follow the Leader* mindsets. As we will see in the following Blockbuster case, leaders who turn their company into a dominant player risk endangering its future if they appoint a *Head in the Sand* CEO who keeps doing what worked in the past – thereby making the company increasingly irrelevant to customers and sending it into bankruptcy.

These implications emerge from examining how the video entertainment industry is changing.

Rapidly evolving technologies for producing, delivering, and displaying images and sound have transformed the video entertainment industry over the last 70 years. In the 1950s, television was a box that displayed black-and-white videos including quiz shows, soap operas, news, and scripted comedies. Until the 1980s, ABC, CBS, and NBC – which started off as radio broadcasters and were granted television licenses by the FCC – produced and distributed free video entertainment to viewers while charging companies to advertise to their captive audiences. By 2013, the audience of these broadcast networks had plunged by two-thirds. HBO, ESPN, CNN, and Nickelodeon won a chunk of that audience by delivering their own programming via coaxial cable. Cable companies monetized their investments by charging monthly fees and selling ads. The Internet and streaming video brought new competitors to the fore. In 2011, Amazon gave away its Instant Video streaming service at no charge to customers who signed up for its Amazon Prime delivery service. YouTube had the most unique visitors, and it made money when viewers opted in to watching ads displayed with the content. Netflix's online streaming service – with its low monthly fee for commercial-free streaming – dominated the new generation of video entertainment by taking advantage of viewers' "managed dissatisfaction with the 20 minutes per hour of traditional television consumed by commercials and promotional messages for other network programming."[1]

Such streaming services were dubbed over-the-top (OTT) media because they delivered video entertainment to consumers without requiring them to pay cable or satellite fees. OTT was a large and rapidly growing market with revenue expected to grow at a 15.2% compound annual rate from $67.8 billion in 2018 (over 10 times the 2010 level) to $158.8 billion in 2024. Netflix dominated the OTT market with an estimated 150 million paying users out of the 180 million US total in December 2019. US-based OTT users spent an estimated 17.5 hours with these services per week in 2019. Surprisingly, OTT users were expected to be more receptive to advertisers who could target their ads more precisely to specific consumer groups.[2] The OTT market attracted numerous rivals. Prior to the November 2019 entry of rivals Disney+ and Apple TV+, Forrester Research analyzed OTT services based on user experience and functionality – concluding that Netflix led the industry on user experience (which included measures of effectiveness, ease, confidence, freedom, and aesthetics), while Hulu prevailed on functionality (meaning problem and account management, content selection, content discovery, and viewing experience). Rivals that trailed these two included Amazon Prime, HBO Go, ESPN+, CBS All Access, and others.[3] In the absence of a major technological innovation – as online streaming was to video stores – the industry was likely to become less profitable due to intense price competition and escalating content investment by rivals seeking to gain market share.

The Covid-19 pandemic led to a surge in demand for video streaming – even as incumbents began to offer their own streaming services. By May 2020, NBC's Peacock and HBO Max were preparing to launch. In April, Quibi launched a ten-minute video service (with disappointing results).[4] Other incumbents acquired their way into video streaming – Viacom bought streaming service Pluto TV; Comcast took control of. XUMO and Fox merged with Tubi, an ad-based video-on-demand platform. These new rivals were entering the industry just as demand for streaming surged – up 12% – a trend expected to continue as consumers were quarantined at home, leading to higher engagement and faster subscriber growth. The surge in demand benefited Netflix in the first quarter of 2020 which added 15.8 million subscribers – about 80% more than J.P. Morgan had estimated.[5] The higher level of demand for streaming services was likely to persist – depending on the pandemic's duration and whether the work-at-home trend continued or abated once the pandemic ended.

Strategic Mindsets of Video Entertainment Industry Winners and Losers

Gaining market share in this rapidly growing industry required leaders to envision and execute an effective competitive strategy to provide an industry-leading consumer experience. Whether a strategy yielded market share gains or losses depended to a large extent on which of the three strategic mindsets – *Create the Future*, *Follow the Leader*, and *Head in the Sand* – the CEO adopted. Here are some general observations based on the collision of these three mindsets with video entertainment industry reality explored in the following case studies:

- **Leaders with *Create the Future* and *Follow the Leader* mindsets are winners:**
    - *Create the Future* works well if leaders are intellectually humble in pursuit of delivering consumers ever more benefits for the money than rivals do. As we will see in the following, Netflix's *Create the Future* mindset was notably distinct from Steve Jobs's mindset at Apple. Jobs envisioned how evolving technology could be harnessed to create new hardware that would delight consumers. Jobs maintained tight control over all aspects of the new products – such as the iPod and the iPhone. By contrast, Netflix's CEO Reed Hastings created similarly revolutionary services – DVD-by-Mail and online streaming. However, he prided himself on delegating much of the decision-making and execution to talented and empowered executives and employees.
    - *Follow the Leader* is a mindset of CEOs who see an upstart's rapid growth and decide to do something about it. In video entertainment, many incumbents have this mindset – seeking a middle ground between

ignoring online streaming and betting the company on a rival online streaming service. In this chapter, we examine one such *Follow the Leader* approach by Hulu – a partnership between rival broadcasters ABC, NBC, Fox, and others – which made some of their old content available to consumers via online streaming. Over time, each partner learned enough about the potential risks and opportunities of online streaming to decide whether to invest in it more heavily or to sell out. Disney emerged as Hulu's dominant owner.

- ***Head in the Sand* leaders preside over failure:** In video entertainment, Blockbuster's demise was due to its *Head in the Sand* mindset. While it did eventually try to create its own versions of Netflix's DVD-by-Mail and online streaming services, Blockbuster was locked into an idea that enabled it to gain a large share of the video store market – by acquiring rivals. The debt Blockbuster took on to pay for those acquisitions ultimately caused it to file for bankruptcy. Ironically, Blockbuster's fate might have been different had it not turned down the opportunity to acquire Netflix before it achieved online streaming market leadership.

Video Entertainment Industry Startup and Incumbent Success and Failure Case Studies

These general observations play out in the following case studies. Netflix's *Create the Future* mindset enabled it to create two new industries – DVD-by-Mail and online streaming – which attracted competition from rivals with a *Follow the Leader* mindset. Hulu, a joint venture of TV incumbents, has progressed to the point that it is a formidable Netflix rival. Collectively, traditional TV industry players are chipping away at Netflix's online streaming market leadership. Leaving unanswered the question of whether Netflix must invent a third new industry to revive its growth in the decade ahead. Meanwhile a *Head in the Sand* mindset contributed to Blockbuster's 2010 demise after it was unable to survive the heavy debt load it took on to acquire video store rivals while responding with too little, too late to Netflix's online streaming threat.

Success: Netflix Twice Creates the Future of Video Entertainment

Introduction

While it is common for companies to come up with one industry-transforming innovation, it is rare for it to come up with a second one in a row. Apple introduced the iPod in 2001 and six years later launched the iPhone which incorporated what the iPod did and added more. The mindset of Steve Jobs – he envisioned where technology and consumers were heading and designed and built handheld devices that would tap into those trends to provide consumers with more benefits – was critical in creating the future of personal technology. Fortunately, Jobs was not the only entrepreneur with such a mindset. Indeed, Netflix's CEO Reed Hastings created the future twice in a row: first by presiding over the successful 1999 launch of its DVD-by-Mail service and in 2007 – after developing a new set of corporate capabilities – introducing an online streaming service that by 2019 had attracted 166 million paying subscribers.[6] Yet Hastings's approach to creating the future differed radically from Jobs's. Unlike Jobs, Hastings did not exercise total personal control over the service's design. He created a culture that attracted excellent talent, gave people the power to make and execute decisions, and held them accountable by widely sharing detailed performance data – including with the board of directors.

Case Scenario

Hastings was a math whiz who started and sold a software company, Pure Software. After exploring numerous startup ideas with Marc Randolph, who was Netflix's first CEO, they settled on the idea of ordering DVDs via the Internet and delivering them from a warehouse directly to consumers' mailboxes. In the decade ending December 2019, Netflix's stock led the S&P 500 – soaring 4,100%, over 21 times faster than the S&P 500's 190% rise.[7] Netflix's success can be traced to Hastings's strategic mindset – based on operating Netflix so that he made very few decisions himself. In a 2018 interview, Hastings said prided himself on making so few decisions that he could go an entire three months without making one. Netflix operated effectively because of one of the most significant decisions he made years before – to give "each employee agency to make their own wise decisions on behalf of the organization." Netflix's most important cultural value was "independent decision-making by employees" – based on a belief that people "thrive on being trusted, on freedom, and on being able to make a difference." Hastings believed that information sharing across Netflix made it the opposite of Apple – which famously compartmentalized information. Netflix also shared far more information with its board of directors than did most companies – whose boards met only four to eight times a year and reviewed dense PowerPoint slides which were controlled tightly by

CEOs. By contrast, Netflix board members attended monthly and quarterly senior management meetings as observers and received 30-page memos full of analysis and data. As a result, Netflix board meetings featured "an intelligent and informed conversation" giving the board the confidence to make hard decisions, according to Hastings.[8] Hastings pre-Netflix experience led him to an intense dislike of process – which he viewed as a "python" that would stifle talent. To that end, Netflix's culture was envisioned as a force for empowering people, giving them a sense of responsibility, and enabling them to operate without chaos – despite the absence of process. Employees seemed to like this – a 2017 study found that Netflix topped the rankings for employee satisfaction and employee pay. Hastings expressed delight that "big decisions at Netflix were made frequently without his input."[9]

Hastings's origin story reveals that he was a math and software aficionado whose experience starting and selling a software venture made him realize that success depended far more on recruiting and motivating the world's best talent than on building an excellent product. He attended private school in Cambridge, Massachusetts; earned an undergraduate degree in math at Bowdoin College; taught high school math in Swaziland; earned a master's degree in computer science from Stanford; and became a Silicon Valley software entrepreneur. In 1991, he started Pure Software, a software debugging program. By 1996, Pure employed 600 people. Hastings gave Pure's product high marks and his management style a far lower one. In 1997, Rational Software acquired Pure Software – and IBM acquired Rational for $700 million. Hastings felt like a failure which led him to an insight – it is better to think more about recruiting and motivating talent than product engineering – which influenced how he ran Netflix. Hastings and Randolph founded Netflix that year to deliver DVD-by-Mail with help from Neil Hunt, who used his math skills to develop software to recommend the next DVD a subscriber should rent based on the subscriber's viewing history. In 1999, Hastings hired Ted Sarandos, a former vice president of product and marketing for video rental store, West Coast Video. Sarandos added to Netflix's product selection, and by 2002, Netflix was profitable and had gone public.[10]

Five years later, Netflix had launched its second act – online streaming to PCs. The new service preceded premature predictions of Netflix's demise at the hands of Walmart's later-aborted DVD-by-Mail service and services offered by Apple and Amazon to download movies to TVs – which did not gain traction with consumers. In January 2007, Netflix delivered its response to those who realized that DVDs were not a "hundred-year format" by launching a service which would enable consumers to stream video to their PCs without downloading and saving it there. Investors panned Netflix's online streaming launch – citing the high investment required to introduce the service, the large number of rivals, and Netflix's lack of competitive advantage (its DVD-by-Mail logistics skill would be of no use). In 2007, Netflix saw two big barriers to widespread adoption of online streaming: technology had not advanced sufficiently to stream and display video quickly and with high visual quality and the reluctance of movie and TV content producers to cannibalize their theater, cable, and advertising revenues. Blockbuster, which had *launched its own DVD-by-Mail service in 2004, was the biggest potential rival to Netflix. Hastings was prescient when he remarked that investors were rightly skeptical of Silicon Valley companies that could not innovate a second "generation of computing."[11] It was not until 2011 that Netflix announced it would do something about its inability to stream new content – spend $100 million to produce 26 episodes of House of Cards. In September 2011, Hastings – who was afraid of being too slow to move away from DVD-by-Mail – blundered by announcing the company would split into two: one offering DVD-by-Mail and the other online streaming. Moreover, Netflix boosted the combined subscription fee by 60%. Subscribers balked and Netflix quickly rescinded the price increase. When House of Cards launched in February 2013, its popularity soared, and Netflix's stock price ended the year three times higher than it had begun.[12]*

By November 2019 when Disney and Apple launched their competitive services, the threat to Netflix's market leadership in online streaming had become palpable. Netflix and YouTube ranked first and second in time spent viewing. However, new services like Disney+, WarnerMedia's HBO Max, and Apple TV+ were expected to erode the dominance of Netflix and YouTube. More specifically, the pair's share of US adults was expected to decline as the average time watching them per day increased. For example, in 2020 eMarketer expected that the average US adult would spend 6% more time – or 29 minutes per day, while its share of daily video time was expected to decline from 27% in 2019 to 25.7% in 2021. eMarketer analyst Ross Benes told Variety, "The video streaming landscape will get crowded, which will drive down the share of time that people devote to Netflix."[13] These crowds threatened Netflix's domestic revenue growth which had risen 122% between 2015 and 2019 with a relatively slow 44% increase in the number of domestic subscribers abetted by a 54% increase in average revenue per user – from about $9/month in 2015 to more than $13/month in 2019. With rivals pricing competitively, Netflix would risk losing more market share if it increased prices. In 2019, only HBO Max ($14.99/month) was more expensive than Netflix. Hulu ($5.99/month), Apple TV+ ($4.99/month), Disney+ ($6.99/month), and Amazon Prime ($8.99/month) all charged less than Netflix did. Meanwhile, Netflix's spending to produce original contact had risen 25% from $12 billion in 2018 to $15 billion in 2019. Competitive pressure would likely cause that investment to rise even faster in future years.[14]

Case Analysis

Reed Hastings achieved the remarkable feat of reinventing the video entertainment industry twice. His approach to creating the future was made all the more interesting because in many ways he did the opposite of what Steve Jobs did in creating the future of personal technologies such as the MP3 player (iPod) and smartphone (iPhone) – the latter playing a key role in the success of Netflix's online streaming. Unlike Jobs, who hoarded control over the design, manufacturing, delivery, and service of its innovations, Hastings was content to hire world-class talent, push responsibility for strategy and execution to those people, and create a culture in which people would take responsibility and be held accountable for their actions. This culture enabled Netflix to reinvent itself as it transitioned from DVD-by-Mail to online streaming. By 2020, competitive pressure from incumbents raised the question of whether Netflix's continued success would depend on reinventing itself a third time.

Success: Hulu Helps Incumbents Hedge Their Bets As They Define Their Futures

Introduction

When a startup introduces a new service that quickly takes on masses of new customers, longtime industry giants are likely to notice. The reaction of these goliaths could range from dismissing the startup as too small to warrant their attention to scrambling to acquire it. Two logical middle ground solutions come to mind for a traditional industry incumbent: each company starts its own service to compete with the upstart or a group of incumbents forms a partnership which starts and operates as a rival to the upstart. Each option has its advantages and disadvantages. The advantage of the first option is that it gives each company control over the destiny of the new service; the disadvantage is that the investment required is relatively large. The second option spreads that investment over all the partners; however, its governance is complicated by the blend of shared and competing interests of all the partners. However, if such a partnership is structured so that participants have clear paths for exiting or investing more deeply based on their different goals and resources, these complications can ultimately be resolved.

Case Scenario

This comes to mind in considering the creation and evolution of Hulu – a joint venture begun in October 2007 between AOL, Comcast, Facebook, MSN, Myspace, and Yahoo – to combat Netflix's then-newly introduced online streaming service.[15] *Initial distribution partners included NBC and Fox (ABC joined in 2009). Hulu – which launched in March 2018 – was a website that streamed then-current and many past television shows which required viewers to watch commercials seen on the broadcasters' websites. Hulu Plus, a service launched in November 2010, delivered more shows, with fewer commercials, on multiple devices – at a price of eight dollars per month. By 2013, Hulu Plus had attracted five million viewers. Despite Hulu's fast growth and $1 billion worth of revenue, Jason Kilar, Hulu's CEO from 2008 to April 2013, quit to start his own venture because Hulu's parent companies resisted his vision – a service which let consumers watch programs at a time convenient for their schedules with few, if any, advertisements.*[16]

Hulu ended 2019 with roughly five times more subscribers and one dominant owner. In the ensuing six years, Hulu's ownership structure became far simpler with Disney emerging as the dominant owner ending 2019 with over five times more subscribers. At that time, Hulu's services included a $5.99/month version with limited advertising, $11.99/month with no advertising, and a $44.99/ month service with no advertising on over 60 live channels. Hulu had 28.5 million subscribers and 2018 advertising revenue of $1.5 billion (up 45% from 2017). Majority-owner Disney projected a 2019 loss of over $1.5 billion[17] and between 40 million and 60 million subscribers by 2024. While Hulu was the only streaming service combining live TV and on-demand, being owned by Disney cost it control of its strategy – for example, in 2019 it lost bidding wars to keep reruns of "Seinfeld" and "South Park."[18] Disney's takeover of Hulu stretched in multiple transactions spanning December 2017 and May 2019. In December 2017, Disney announced a deal to acquire 21st Century Fox. By the deal's close in March 2018, Disney's stake in Hulu doubled to 60% – as it added Fox's 30% share. In March 2019, AT&T sold its 9.5% share in Hulu back to Disney for $1.43 billion. In May 2019, Comcast also gave up its shares of Hulu to Disney while maintaining a 33% Hulu stake through NBCUniversal.[19]

By the end of 2019, Hulu had announced that it would raise prices to offset the rising costs of producing live TV. However, its role within Disney remained a work in process. In December 2019, Hulu raised the price for its Hulu + Live TV offering by $10 a month to $55. While growing rapidly, researcher MoffettNathanson estimated in November 2019 that Hulu + Live TV's subscriber count had more than doubled to 2.7 million from 1.2 million the year before. However, Disney's losses were also skyrocketing. Losses at its direct-to-consumer and international segments more than doubled to $740 million in its fiscal fourth quarter. Hulu was expected to house older and original programming from FX networks. Disney introduced that month a bundle – including Disney+, ESPN+, and ad-supported Hulu – for $12.99 a month. Ten million people had signed up including those using its seven-day free trial.[20]

Case Analysis

Over the course of 12 years, Hulu's ownership and strategy evolved, and its subscriber based grew rapidly. Yet during that same timespan, Netflix had more five and a half times the number of subscribers. Both companies attracted these subscribers while losing billions. The relatively slow growth of Hulu reflects the way the mindset of an established incumbent – trying to sort out differences with other incumbents – slows down the process of setting and executing growth strategy. With Disney emerging as the dominant owner of Hulu, decisions and execution are likely to speed up – yet still be impeded by potential conflicts between Hulu, Disney+, and Disney's other entertainment businesses.

Failure: Blockbuster Goes Bankrupt As Debt-Fueled Deal Doing Delays Its Response to Industry Changes

Introduction

Innovators often perish when they stop innovating. More specifically, a company that invents a new product or service that gains popularity often adapts poorly to the later emergence of an even better product or service. A case in point is Digital Equipment Corporation (DEC), a Massachusetts company that invented the minicomputer, which grew popular with organizations that were frustrated by the high cost and inflexibility of mainframe computers. DEC did well for decades until the 1980s when PCs emerged. DEC CEO Ken Olson could not understand why people would need PCs, and his inability to adapt effectively to the growing popularity of the PC led it to be acquired by Compaq, a PC industry leader, in 1998.[21] DEC's failure to adapt highlights three essential conditions that often impede innovators from adapting to a new wave of technology:

- **CEO confirmation bias:** Leaders develop mental models to explain and communicate how they achieved their initial success. Often these mental models ascribe the success to the CEO's superior talents – while underweighting the importance of luck. Nevertheless, these mental models shape the way leaders process information – causing them to seek and accept information that reinforces their mental models and reject information that contradicts them. Such confirmation bias makes it difficult for CEOs to adapt well to change.
- **Failure to see the company through the customer's eyes:** Confirmation bias can prevent a CEO from viewing the company from the customer's perspective. For example, when the PC became popular – as office workers used it to create documents or create spreadsheets – Olson was unable to perceive how much more valuable the PC was to workers who used DEC's minicomputers. He viewed the minicomputer as the ultimate product and ignored evidence from consumers that the PC could be a better value – by providing consumers with far greater benefits for the price.
- **Inability to create new capabilities:** Confirmation bias can also block leaders from recognizing that to take advantage of new opportunities, they must develop new capabilities. For example, as we saw earlier in this

chapter, Netflix was able to develop new capabilities – such as creating its own popular shows and partnering with broadband service providers – to be successful in online streaming. At the same time, it jettisoned some of the people who were essential to its DVD-by-Mail business – who ordered, stored, and retrieved DVDs – as demand for its original service declined. Leaders beset with confirmation bias are often so slow to recognize the need to add new capabilities and subtract some old ones, that their response comes too late to keep the company from failing.

This comes to mind in considering Blockbuster – which rented out videocassettes and DVDs in thousands of stores around the United States and perished in 2010 as Netflix's combination of DVD-by-Mail and online streaming took away too many of Blockbuster's customers. While Blockbuster had a string of owners and CEOs, they all seemed to share the same deal-oriented mindset which impeded the company from inventing new services that customers would value more than Netflix and other competing services.

Case Scenario

Blockbuster was founded in 1985 by an oil services equipment distributor. 25 years and five CEOs later, it filed for bankruptcy. While Blockbuster's journey was full of interesting twists and turns, its failure was ultimately the result of its loss of leadership in the business of supplying video entertainment to consumers. In 1978, that database expert, David Cook, founded Cooks Data, a supplier of tools and software to Texan oil and gas companies. In the mid-1980s, the oil market collapsed, and Cook's wife pushed him to enter the video rental market. In October 1985, he opened the first Blockbuster store in Dallas. After the collapse of the oil market in the mid-1980s, Cook, at the urging of his wife, decided to try his luck in the video rental market. He opened the first Blockbuster store in Dallas in October of 1985. Blockbuster grew quickly because it offered consumers a family-friendly atmosphere with longer operating hours, wider selection (8,000 VHS tapes in over 6,500 titles) displayed on shelves instead of behind the counter, and more efficient checkout via a computer system and scanner. Cook wanted capital to grow Blockbuster, but an article questioning his knowledge of the industry quashed a public stock offering planned for September 1986. Losing over $3 million, in February 1987, Cook sold a third of the company to Waste Management founder, Wayne Huizenga, and other investors for over $18 million. Huizenga bought more of the company and abandoned Cook's strategy of growth through franchising in favor of acquiring Blockbuster's competitors.[22]

Huizenga's acquisition strategy achieved rapid growth – but ultimately overstepped the limits of what the company could afford. The first murmur of trouble came in May 1989 when investment analysts at the now-defunct Bear Stearns called

Blockbuster's accounting practices "inaccurate and grossly misleading." Though Blockbuster refused to change its accounting practices, its largest shareholder, United Artists Entertainment, dumped its 12% stake and sold its 28 franchised stores. But analysts noted that the industry was maturing fast – while in 1988 monthly Blockbuster revenue growth was 35%, in 1989 and 1990 growth plunged to around 8% each year. Huizenga decided to look globally for growth. By 1993, Blockbuster had over 3,400 stores and was acquiring music retailers such as Sound Warehouse and Music Plus to broaden its product line. He envisioned Blockbuster as an entertainment center that would rent movies and sell music, computer programs, video games, and virtual reality entertainment. In September 1993, Blockbuster bid offered to pay $4.7 billion for Viacom which was in a bidding war with QVC for Paramount. By the time it was over, Viacom had acquired Blockbuster for $8.4 billion.[23]

Blockbuster went on to suffer plunging cash flow under the supervision of three CEOs – one a year between 1994 and 1997. Huizenga left in September 1994; next up was Blockbuster President Steven Berrard who left after 18 months to be replaced by Walmart Executive Bill Fields who lasted until spring 1997 – three months before John Antioco took over. Antioco faced the challenge of turning around a company whose cash flow tumbled 70% in the second quarter of 1997 as new releases were not getting to stores. He tried to right the ship by cutting people, selling Blockbuster Music, shutting international stores, and exiting the PC business. Viacom had acquired Blockbuster hoping that its cash flow would help finance the money it borrowed to acquired Paramount. Instead Viacom was injecting cash into Blockbuster and tried to minimize the damage by offering 18% of Blockbuster in what turned out to be a disappointing public stock offering.[24]

This furious financially focused deal making distracted Blockbuster from technological and business trends that would ultimately drive video stores out of existence. The rapidly growing Internet was making it easier for consumers to obtain videos ordered from their PCs – without requiring them to pay late fees. Amazon had moved from selling books to DVDs online; Netflix introduced its DVD-by-Mail service. Despite forming partnerships with AOL, TiVo, and DIRECTV to explore streaming video and home delivery of DVDs, it was not until August 2004 that Blockbuster introduced its own DVD rental program. In the interim, Blockbuster turned down a spring 2000 chance to acquire 49% of Netflix – which was then losing money and had a mere 300,000 subscribers. Hastings offered to change Netflix's name to Blockbuster.com and operate Blockbuster's online service. Blockbuster declined the offer since it did not yet see a threat from digital media.[25] *In December 2004, Blockbuster was itching to make a hostile bid to acquire its biggest rival, the now-defunct Hollywood Video. Greenmailer Carl Icahn decided that this deal needed to be done, so he bought about ten million shares of Blockbuster. But in January 2005, Hollywood Video accepted an offer from Movie Gallery.*[26]

Icahn's entry led to Antioco's departure who was replaced by James Keyes, former head of 7-Eleven, who presided over Blockbuster's 2010 bankruptcy filing. Icahn got himself onto Blockbuster's board and challenged Antioco's huge pay package. Icahn *also pushed Antioco – who wanted to end late fees and transform Blockbuster into an online video store – to sell the company to a private equity firm. Antioco left in 2007 and Keyes took over as CEO. Keyes cut costs, changed Blockbuster's service, and achieved growth and profitability by pushing its online and digital services. Sadly, for Keyes, by the time he took over in 2007, Blockbuster had borrowed more than it could repay. Its $400 million line of credit expired, and the financial crisis took hold – contributing to its uncertainty about whether by September 30, 2009, Blockbuster would be able to make a $42 million payment on its $1 billion in debt.*[27] *A year later, still operating 3,300 stores, Blockbuster filed for bankruptcy.*[28]

Case Analysis

When the only tool you know how to use is a hammer, every problem becomes a nail. This is essentially the problem that Blockbuster faced – one which became fatal after it borrowed too much money to acquire other chains of video stores. While its first CEO, Cook, had a *Create the Future* mindset – harnessing database technology to give customers a better video store experience – his successor, Huizenga, knew one thing: growth through acquisition. The imperatives of doing deals and paying back the debt borrowed to finance them were of preeminent importance. Blockbuster's leadership – which sprang from Cook's ability to stay ahead of changing technology and evolving customer needs[29] – was lost the day he ceded control of the company to Huizenga.

Video Entertainment Industry Case Study Takeaways

The takeaways from these case studies have varying implications depending on where you sit.

Incumbent Executives

- **Do:** Based on the Netflix and Hulu cases, bricks and mortar executives may create competitive advantage by
  - Creating a culture that attracts, empowers, and holds accountable world-class talent in functions that are critical to the company's success
  - Experimenting with a new business model that monetizes a content library to gather data on whether to invest further in its development
  - Choosing which customers to target for their services and using data analytics to evaluate which specific content will attract the most subscribers

- Partnering with talented producers, writers, actors, and others to produce such content
- Investing in technology – based on factors such as Forrester's user experience and functionality – to enhance the quality of their target customers' online streaming service
- Using knowledge of their customer's buying behavior and unmet needs to develop industry-transforming new services

- **Do not:** Based on the Blockbuster case, bricks and mortar executives should avoid its self-destructive tactics such as
    - Minimizing the strategic significance of an upstart's rapidly growing service and delaying the introduction of a competing service
    - Placing a higher priority on growth through a previously successful but now-outmoded strategy than on observing and responding to changing consumer behavior and new technology
    - Borrowing extensively to execute the outmoded growth strategy
    - Making the company vulnerable to activist investors by endangering its financial condition

Incumbent Employees

- **Do:** Based on the Netflix and Hulu cases, incumbent employees may seek to stay at the incumbent based on whether
    - The CEO seeks to invest in a video streaming service that leads the industry in the quality of its content and delivery, ease of navigation and use, and price.
    - The company's culture attracts world-class talent and empowers the talent to innovate.
- **Do not:** Based on the Blockbuster and Hulu cases, incumbent employees should consider seeking employment elsewhere if the company's CEO
    - Focuses on borrowing too much money in pursuit of a now-outmoded growth strategy
    - Straddles an effort to protect an old declining business while investing cautiously in creating a new one

Startup CEOs

- **Do:** Based on the Netflix and Hulu cases, Startup CEOs may scale their companies by
  - Creating a culture that attracts and inspires talented people to capture growth opportunities
  - Investing in a new service that provides customers with industry-leading quality of content and delivery, ease of navigation and use, and price
  - Investing in or partnering with a provider of consumer hardware that delivers a much higher-quality viewing experience than do HD TVs, smartphones, and/or tablets
- **Do not:** Based on the Blockbuster case, Startup CEOs should avoid its self-destructive tactics such as
  - Diminishing the significance of fast-growing rivals with different business strategies
  - Acquiring companies or building products based on what the CEO believes without listening to customers

Business Students

- **Do:** Based on the Netflix and Hulu cases, business students may seek employment with companies that
  - Create a culture in which top talent is encouraged to take responsibility for innovation and generate measurable benefits for customers
  - Invest in new services that will provide consumers with superior content, wider selection, and excellent transmission and image quality
- **Do not:** Based on the Blockbuster case, business students should avoid companies that
  - Seek to preserve a declining business while starving new services for resources
  - Place a higher emphasis on quarterly financial results than on investing in growth opportunities that will pay off in the longer term

Do You Have the Strategic Mindset of a Video Entertainment Industry Winner?

If you answer in the affirmative to these questions, you have a winning strategic mindset. If not, you must decide whether to change your mindset, strategy, and execution or find a job that better suits your strengths and interests:

- Do you know what delights your customers about buying from your company?
- Are you providing your customers an ever-improving video entertainment experience?
- Does your company have a compelling culture that attracts talented people?
- Do you encourage your people to take responsibility for conceiving and implementing innovations that benefit customers?

Conclusion

The video entertainment industry is large and growing rapidly. This growth is creating opportunity for upstarts and many incumbents. The incumbents have considerable financial resources and libraries of old content – some of which can be streamed online to generate new revenue. Netflix – which is an upstart in the minds of traditional TV broadcasters – has created two generations of industry-dominating business models. However, the slow emergence of competing services from incumbents who have followed the leader may impinge on Netflix's growth. It remains to be seen whether Netflix's unique culture can spawn a third industry-transforming innovation that again leaves slow-moving followers in the dust. In Chapter 4, we will examine how such interactions play out in the newspaper industry.

CHAPTER

4

Newspapers

With the rise of social media and digital advertising, the newspaper industry was in decline in 2019, and Covid-19 accelerated the decline. Sadly, for newspapers that had not built a substantial online subscription base, severe cost cutting was not expected to offset the plunge in advertising revenue from small- and medium-sized enterprises whose revenues were reduced by social distancing. Without a significant infusion of additional capital, most traditional newspapers would not be able to accelerate their online subscriptions enough to become sustainable. Simply put, the fate of many newspapers depended on whether they could persuade private equity firms to acquire them: yet as we will see later in this chapter, exiting the industry in this way cost many jobs and transferred to the new owners the dwindling cash flows from an aging population of print newspaper subscribers. Absent transferring newspapers to private equity or other financial buyers, liquidation appeared to be a likely fate for many newspapers.

These implications emerge from examining the performance and prospects of the most difficult industry covered in this book. Newspaper subscription and advertising revenues were declining as were the industry's employee base and its profitability. A handful of the largest newspapers were achieving considerable success signing up digital subscribers; however, the subscription and digital advertising rates were much lower than traditional newspaper subscription and print advertising rates. Private equity firms were acquiring these dying newspaper chains and raising the rates on print subscriptions to harvest the unwillingness of older readers to switch to digital media consumption. Meanwhile, Google and Facebook made news available to users at no charge while operating digital advertising platforms that enabled advertisers to

P. S. Cohan, *Goliath Strikes Back*, https://doi.org/10.1007/978-1-4842-6519-2_4

generate much higher returns on their marketing budgets than print ads previously did. Prospects for the newspaper industry were so bleak that longtime newspaper industry bull, Warren Buffett, sold his newspapers in early 2020 (providing high rate debt to finance the deal).

The data supporting this pessimistic outlook were compelling. Total newspaper industry revenue dropped at a five-year average annual rate of 4.3% between 2014 and 2019 to $24.5 billion. During that period, the number of employees in the industry fell at a 3.3% annual rate, the number of independent newspapers fell at a 1.5% annual rate, and print advertising fell far more quickly at a 6.2% annual rate. Meanwhile, circulation tumbled at 7.7% in 2018 – the most recent year available. Industry employment fell at a 7.2% rate to 144,544 workers during the period – yet the cost cutting could not halt the decline in average profit margins from an 7.3% of revenue in 2014 to 5% in 2019. Underlying these statistics was an industry which had not adapted quickly enough to new technologies introduced by Google, Facebook, and other upstarts. Online media made it far more compelling for most consumers to migrate to online content, and advertisers followed them. Newspapers lost what had been their most important source of revenue – print circulation and advertising – which captured a declining share of advertising budgets. Perhaps the sole source of optimism for print newspapers was the loyalty to print of older and more affluent subscribers who were willing to pay a higher price to continue to receive printed news.[1]

While Google and Facebook accounted for most digital advertising revenue – controlling 86% of all online advertising growth in 2017[2] – Craigslist (founded in 1995) was the first to siphon advertising from newspapers. Craigslist ran a network of usually free websites advertising jobs, housing, personals, and items for sale which by September 2012 had expanded into 70 countries. Its founder Craig Newmark recognized that consumers were frustrated that newspapers expected them to pay by the line for an advertisement that would be buried among other tiny notices that would be difficult for buyers to search. Craigslist offered consumers quicker, mostly free matches with sellers via email (rather than waiting a day for the classified to be printed).[3] As smartphone adoption surged between 2014 and 2019, digital content producers drew readers and advertising revenue from newspapers. Although readership grew through newspapers' online editions, the much lower digital pricing did not offset the loss of more-valuable print subscribers.[4]

Digital advertising increased not only because it followed readers from print to smartphone but also because of its advantages for advertisers. These included digital advertising's ability to personalize promotional messages to consumers based on demographic information and prior browsing activity. As Dan Kennedy, Associate Professor of Journalism at Northeastern, explained in a February 2020 interview, "More than anything, the collapse of newspaper revenues can be attributed to monumental shifts in advertising. Classified ads accounted for 40% of a typical newspaper's revenues not that many years ago, but nearly all of it was scooped up by Craigslist." Digital advertising was not as compelling to readers as was print. "Display advertising did not make a successful transition to digital — rather than something that looked like print advertising, which many readers regarded as attractive and useful, we got annoying banner ads, pop-ups and pop-unders. Finally, more than 90% of all new spending on digital advertising has gone to Google and Facebook in recent years," Kennedy said.[5]

Advertisers seeking to reach readers online had many options and were disaffected by the lower level of reader engagement with digital content. Therefore, newspapers set lower rates and earned lower digital advertising revenue.[6] Chuck Plunkett, Director of University of Colorado Boulder's News Corp who was formerly editorial page editor of *The Denver Post*, told me in a February 2020 interview that Google advertising is more effective. As Plunkett explained, "Their ability to micro-target is key for advertisers. I know that Facebook is constantly showing me a cool niche clothing outlet. They somehow just KNOW my interests. Same with Google ads. Most news advertising isn't that sophisticated." Most online newspaper sites irritated him. "I can't read some stories for the annoying way ads keep popping up to stop my reading and viewing experience. Too many sites have videos that start playing whether you want to hear them or not. And dear God the requests that you sign up for a newsletter! It can be like running the gauntlet at some sites just to read a tiny little story."[7]

By 2020, the newspaper industry's next five years looked even worse – featuring further declines in revenue, employment, number of independent institutions, and profitability. By 2024, industry revenue was projected to fall at an average 2.9% annual rate to $21.2 billion, the number of industry employees was expected to drop at a 3.3% annual rate to 122,032, and the number of newspapers was anticipated to decline at a 2.1% rate to 3,689. A significant reason for the decline was the expected 4% annual drop in print advertising budgets during the period.[8] The largest newspapers – such as *The New York Times, The Wall Street Journal*, and *The Washington Post* – created paywalls which required users to pay if they wanted to read more than a minimum number of digital articles each month. By May 2019, the Times had 3.4 million digital subscribers (who paid $15/month); the Journal's 1.7 million digital subscribers paid $39/month, and the Post's 1.5 million were charged $10/month.[9] Such newspapers also generated additional revenue from so-called native advertising – stories written in the tone of a news report coupled with a disclaimer that they were paid for by the advertiser. The publications then pushed traffic to the sponsored message to boost value for the advertiser.

Smaller newspapers which could not benefit from such strategies were acquired by hedge funds (Fortress Investment Group provided capital to New Media which merged with Gannett in 2020) or private equity firms (such as

Alden Capital which invested in MNG the parent of *The Denver Post* and *San Jose Mercury News*). Dean Singleton, who founded MediaNews, the predecessor of MNG, said after his departure, "What Alden is doing is liquidating. They are taking the cash out as quickly as they can and reinvesting in businesses [that] they think have more promise. It may be a very good business strategy, but it is not a good newspaper strategy." MNG said its goal was to make newspapers sustainable, not close them.[10] Such financial owners cut costs – including newsroom staff – while raising the price of print subscriptions. The 53-year-old Plunkett said "it's folks my age and older, and generally folks who are much older, who continue to seek the print experience. Alden knows this. They know they can charge lofty print subscriptions to those of us who wish to have a local paper and they can make steady profits for a few more years. Alden is currently asking $364 a year for its print subscription. The online rate is $65. Why? Beyond the fact print costs money to produce and deliver, the online price is about as much as the company can expect to make."[11] These investors were dedicated to maximizing the ever-shortening lifetime value of these print subscribers.

Warren Buffett announced in April 2019 that he thought the newspaper industry was "toast." In January 2020, Buffett announced the sale of Berkshire's newspaper holding for $140 million to Lee Enterprises.[12] "The things that are essentially news is what you don't know that you want to know." As Buffett said, "You know what happened in national sports the moment it happened, and you can go watch a video of it and so on. You can go to ESPN and see what is going on. You know what is happening in politics. You know what is happening in the stock market. Ads are news to people. It was 'survival of the fattest.' Whichever paper was the fattest won because it had the most ads in it. And ads are news to people. They want to know what supermarkets have the bargain on Coke or Pepsi this weekend and so on. I mean, it upsets the people in the newsroom to talk that way, but the ads were the most important editorial content from the standpoint of the reader. If you were looking for a job, you had one place to basically look, and that was the classified section. If you were looking for an apartment to rent, those pages were just dozens and dozens of pages. That's disappeared. The world was changed hugely, and it did it gradually. It went from monopoly to franchise to competitive to ... toast."[13]

By April 2020, the pandemic had plunged the newspaper industry into even deeper trouble. Newspaper industry revenues were tanking, and workers were losing their jobs as local businesses reduced advertising budgets. MAGNA, an advertising research firm, projected print advertising to decline at least 25% in 2020 – worse than the prepandemic forecast of a 17% decline. Analysts expected many local papers to go out of business. Craig Huber, CEO and founder of Huber Research Partners, an independent equity research firm, anticipated even bigger advertising revenue declines – at least 35%. In the first half of April 2020, dozens of local publications furloughed or laid off reporters, reduced the frequency of their publishing, or dropped their print editions altogether, according to the nonprofit group PEN America. Gannett, the largest newspaper chain in the United States with 261 newspapers in 46 states, warned in April that it expected its revenues to be "significantly impacted by the Covid-19 pandemic" due to declines in advertising and events. To reduce its cash burn rate, Gannett aimed to cut $100 million to $125 million through layoffs and furloughs, significant pay reductions for senior management, and cancellation of nonessential travel and spending.[14]

Strategic Mindsets of Newspaper Industry Winners and Losers

In the shrinking newspaper industry, the difference between success and failure was particularly stark – depending on the company's mindset. Google, a company that exemplified a *Create the Future* mindset better than almost any other, came from outside and slashed the newspaper industry's growth and profitability. By reinventing web search and advertising, Google offered readers and advertisers far more compelling value propositions than did any newspaper industry incumbent. The slow response of *The New York Times* – which took about 16 years to mount an effective digital strategy – exemplified the considerable business risk facing newspapers with a *Follow the Leader* mindset. Most newspapers operated with a *Head in the Sand* mindset – speeding into bankruptcy or getting acquired by a financial buyer seeking to strip out valuable assets, cut costs, and raise prices on print subscriptions and advertising to a dwindling population of elderly readers willing to pay to preserve their newspaper-reading habits. Here are some general observations based on how these three mindsets played out in the newspaper industry which we will explored in the case studies that follow:

- **Executives with a *Create the Future* mindset were winners:** Executives who had extensive careers in the newspaper industry lacked a *Create the Future* mindset. As we will see in the following Google case, it took executives from outside the industry to create its future by applying state-of-the-art technology to capture reader's attention more effectively than did newspapers and enable advertisers to track how well their marketing messages motivated customers to buy.
- **Companies with a *Follow the Leader* mindset boosted their chances of surviving; however, success often depended on hiring an outside CEO:** While most newspapers lacked the scale to support a world-class digital news service, a handful of national

newspapers did. However, because so many of them were led by executives with a long history in the newspaper industry, they often sought growth by acquiring other newspapers and cutting overlapping costs rather than adopting the state-of-the-art technologies Google used to capture readers' attention and advertiser's marketing budgets. While leading national newspapers recognized the need to create such digital services, it took outside executives to overcome the internal opposition to this change in strategy. This was a critical reason why *The New York Times* built a significant digital subscription business as we will see in the case below.

- ***Head in the Sand* leaders were likely to lose their corporate independence:** Many newspapers lost their independence – with the pace of consolidation accelerating following the rise of the Web and the financial crisis of 2008. Newspapers that responded to declining advertising and subscriber revenue by cutting costs – including newsroom staff – simply accelerated their revenue drop and were no longer able to operate sustainably. Many lost their independence and found themselves at the mercy of owners whose ambitions extended beyond the now-quaint idea of serving the local community. By failing to anticipate change, these *Head in the Sand* newspapers were gobbled up by financial buyers.

Newspaper Industry Startup and Incumbent Success and Failure Case Studies

These general observations play out in the following case studies. Google's *Create the Future* mindset enabled it to improve the quality of web search engines and to build an advertising platform that boosted advertisers' return on marketing. Since newspapers chose not to compete against such digital advertising platforms, Google siphoned much of their subscription and advertising revenue. *The New York Times*'s *Follow the Leader* mindset slowly (e.g., after about 16 years) enabled it to build a substantial digital subscription business by hiring more journalists and producing world-class digital content. This strategy did not take root until the *Times* hired an outsider to lead the charge. Meanwhile, a *Head in the Sand* mindset contributed to *The Denver Post*'s loss of its independence in 1980. Although its new owners – Times Mirror and later MediaNews – made investments in the Post's printing facilities and local journalism, neither owner was able to make the Post profitable. The Post's parent went bankrupt in 2010 and continued to operate with a significantly reduced newsroom staff.

Success: Google's Domination of Digital Advertising Eats the Newspaper Industry

Introduction

Google's dominance of search and digital advertising was a powerful example of how a *Create the Future* mindset can capture value from an industry's incumbents. Google's cofounders Sergey Brin and Larry Page built better ways to search the Web and market to consumers. These technologies created irresistibly better value for newspaper readers and advertisers – siphoning away enormous chunks of revenue and profit from the newspaper industry. By February 2020, the company they started in 1996 had grown from an idea to a $162 billion in revenue colossus growing at 20% with 104,000 employees and a stock market value of more than $1 trillion. While Google's rise to dominance was a result of many products that it built and operated, the most significant ones were its world-beating search and digital advertising platforms.

Brin and Page turned Page's Stanford doctoral thesis topic into a better search engine. They met in 1995 when Brin (who had entered the Stanford PhD program in 1993) gave Page a tour of the campus and San Francisco. The two disagreed over many topics – yet they decided to collaborate. Beginning in January 1996, they wrote a program for a search engine called Backrub. At the time, search engines such as AltaVista and Inktomi ranked search results by counting the number of times that the search term appeared on a web page. That approach was vulnerable to spammers who gamed the system by filling their pages with commonly searched keywords (often in barely legible text at the bottom of the page). Backrub returned much more relevant results because its PageRank technology – that analyzed the number and importance of the links to a website – was more difficult to hack. Brin and Page received positive feedback from the Stanford community which both created more demand for Backrub and helped them scrounge up the computing resources they needed to meet that demand. They changed Backrub's name to Google, and after failing to license their search engine technology, Brin and Page decided to build a business around it. They received one of its first checks – for $100,000 – from Sun Microsystems cofounder Andy Bechtolsheim (other angel investors included Amazon CEO Jeff Bezos). Brin and Page incorporated in September 1998 and then launched and answered 10,000 search queries every day.[15] On August 20, 2004, the company sold its shares to the public at about $54 a share in an initial public offering. By February 21, 2020, those shares had increased in value by 27,090%.[16]

Case Scenario

Six years after Google went public, its leadership in digital advertising had enabled it and peers like Facebook to overtake the newspaper industry's decades-long control of the print advertising market. By 2020, Google dominated both print and online advertising. Google's eventual market leadership was not obvious back in 1996 when Brin and Page started the company. In fact, for years they were burning through cash and had no obvious way to generate revenue. They remedied this problem a few years before going public by improving on a digital advertising concept from rival GoTo.com – the first critical step in Google's journey to gobble up the newspaper industry. To be sure, complacency contributed to newspapers' decline. In the second half of the twentieth century, newspapers in the United States made money mainly by selling ads. In 1997, the average operating profit margin of American newspapers was 19.5%, while USA Today publisher Gannett's operating margin was a much higher 26.6%. That did not last. By 2010, Gannett's operating margin had plunged to 6.1%, and in 2019 it was merged out of existence. Much of that loss was initially due to a drop in classified advertising as consumers switched from newspapers to Craigslist. By 2010, web advertising had reached $25.8 billion – surpassing newspaper ad spending for the first time, by $100 million. Google was the biggest force driving web advertising – which was expected to grow nearly 16% in 2011 – accounting for 40% of that forecast.[17] By 2020, Google's ad business was expected to surpass 20% of all US ad spending both online and offline – representing 74.6% of US search ad spending.

How did Google achieve this dominant position in the advertising industry? The short answer is a combination of newspaper executives' efforts to avoid scrapping the investments that had protected their profitability for decades and Google's ability to offer consumers and advertisers much greater benefit for the money than did the newspapers. Newspapers enjoyed local monopolies due to the high fixed costs of newspaper production and distribution (e.g., printing presses, warehouses, reporters, delivery trucks) and low marginal costs for the paper and ink needed to produce the paper. Until the Web became popular, those barriers to entry blocked new rivals and enabled the newspapers to bundle political news, investigative journalism, opinion, sports, local business, employment, and classified advertising. The Internet unbundled these pieces and made them available to consumers and advertisers in ways that were demonstrably easier to use and less costly. For example, Facebook and Twitter were among the many sources of free news and commentary, Google and Facebook took over local advertising, Indeed and others posted employment ads, and OkCupid and Tinder were among the leaders in evaporating newspapers' personal ads. Google supplied advertisers with more efficient self-service platforms and quickly gained market share – abetted by an ambitious acquisition strategy. Between 2004 and 2014, Google spent at least $23 billion buying 145 companies, including digital advertising leader DoubleClick.[18]

While Google had successfully reinvented search, it operated for about two years without generating significant revenue. By the end of 1999, its investors were getting worried. However, after Brin and Page met with Bill Gross, founder of GoTo.com, they began an epic reinvention of digital advertising which remains the core of their business. GoTo.com realized that advertisers were willing to pay for a search engine to return their website in the top position in response to a consumer's search. Gross's solution was to supply advertisers with pay-per-click search ads through an auction system that would allow advertisers to bid up prices for the most relevant search terms. Brin and Page – who disliked key details in the GoTo.com approach – developed what they thought was a better system. In late 2000, Google introduced AdWords, a new, self-service advertising product that allowed businesses to purchase text ads on search-results pages. Soon after, Page and Brin met with Gross at a TED Conference where Gross suggested a merger. Brin and Page turned down Gross because his company – renamed Overture – placed its auction-based ads next to Google's own results (Brin and Page disliked this juxtaposition because it could be gamed if advertisers purchased spammy or off-topic keywords). While a partnership would have benefited Overture by enabling it to maintain the revenue from its Yahoo and MSN partnerships, Google rejected the proposal. In 2002, Google launched AdWords Select – its own pay-per-click, auction-based search-advertising product. This was so successful that Google dropped the original AdWords. Google solved the juxtaposition problem by adding a quality score to each ad that would punish the spammy keywords. Google also improved on Overture's standard high-bid auction model with a variant on the so-called Vickrey auction that kept the winning bidder from overpaying.[19] While Yahoo ended up acquiring Overture for $1.65 billion, Google went on to build another advertising platform called AdSense which sold targeted ads on third-party websites.[20]

By 2019, Google dominated – with a 27% share – the $130 billion digital advertising market by controlling almost every step between advertisers and websites for purchasing and selling digital ads. Google managed this process for ads intended to run on Google's own platforms or sites around the Web. With 80% of the US market for search ads, Google enabled marketers to bid for ads on search-result pages based on phrases that users typed into the Google search bar – through Google Ads (the former AdWords). Advertisers used Google's leading Analytics 360 product to measure the effectiveness of their ad campaigns. Google led the industry in placing ads that appear from most places on the Web – including news and cooking sites, mobile apps, and games. Google enabled marketers to place other kinds of ads such as display ads (banner images in small boxes within or next to articles) or ads within videos. Google also operated Display & Video 360 (DV 360) – the leading tool to purchase ad space. Using DV 360 brands could enter bids to reach web users with specific demographic profiles and interests. The bids were fed through automated electronic auctions – including Google's industry leading (50% market share) AdX – across thousands of websites. Meanwhile, publishers made ad space available on ad marketplaces through ad servers. Google led the publisher ad *serving market with an estimated 70% market share. Google provided specific services for different publishers: large (DoubleClick for Publishers), small (AdSense), and mobile app (AdMob).*[21]

Google's strong market share in digital advertising did not exempt it from the digital advertising slowdown resulting from the pandemic – in 2020, the US digital ad market was expected to eke out a 0.2% gain to $134.7 billion by the end of 2020. Indeed, by June 2020, Google was expected to suffer its first decline in annual advertising sales for the year. Research firm eMarketer forecast a 5.3% decline in Google ad revenue to $39.6 billion. Moreover, Google's market share – while still ending 2020 in the lead – was expected to drop from 31.5% to 29.4%. A reason for the decline was Google's dependence on advertising from industries particularly slowed by the pandemic – including hotels and airlines – which were recovering by June yet slashing their prices to bring back customers. Meanwhile, Amazon – which pulled ecommerce ads from Google – and Facebook were expected to enjoy an increase in ad revenue since they were less dependent on travel industry revenue. More specifically, Amazon was expected to enjoy a 23.5% ad revenue pop, while Facebook ad sales – helped by fast-growing Instagram – was expecting a 4.9% boost in ad revenue.[22]

Case Analysis

Google created the future of web search and advertising. When newspapers were started, the Web did not exist. Its rapid growth in the 1990s caught the newspaper industry by surprise. Newspaper executives had enjoyed decades of undisturbed local monopolies or duopolies which offered high profits and influence. Rather than see Google as a threat (giving readers free content and advertisers a much higher return on their marketing investments), newspapers dismissed Google's significance. Their delayed recognition of Google's superior value proposition to readers and advertisers cost many newspapers their independence. While a handful of the largest newspapers survived by launching effective digital strategies, most have gone bankrupt, sold out to financial buyers, or scramble to survive by cutting costs and struggling to build significant digital revenues. Even capitalist superhero, Warren Buffett, could not figure out how to save local newspapers, so he sold his interests for a pittance. By February 2020, the continued transfer of value from newspapers to Google shareholders appeared unstoppable.

Success: *The New York Times* Creates $800 Million Digital Business

Introduction

When a newspaper that is a national institution suffers drops in revenue and profit, it signals that something is deeply wrong with the industry and possibly with that institution's top executives. When that institution has been trying – and failing – for 16 years to grow faster, that concern is amplified. This comes to mind in considering the condition in which *The New York Times* found itself in 2012. On and off over the previous 16 years, the *Times* tried to introduce a digital service to readers and advertisers – as it tried to reorient itself so that the new technologies and business models that had been costing the newspaper its revenues could instead become a source of growth. This shift in strategy raised difficult questions: was the revenue potential of digital subscriptions and digital advertising large enough to offset the decline in print subscription and advertising? With no prior experience on which to rely, could the *Times* successfully implement a strategy of growth in digital and harvesting print? Would customers and advertisers find the digital services compelling enough to boost the *Times's* revenues sufficiently? These were some of the challenges facing Mark Thompson when he joined the *Times* as CEO in November 2012. Right before he joined, the *Times's* quarterly advertising revenue had fallen 9%, and net income plunged over 80% from the year before – driving its stock price down 22%. Thompson's response was to reorganize and shift the *Times* culture. More specifically, he created a separate division to house the newspaper's print products and services and announced his intention to build a significant digital subscription business. Rather than following the prevailing cost-cutting strategy, Thompson chose to "invest in great content," noting that "the future of journalism is to make more journalism ... and then figure out smart ways to put that in front of people and asking them to support [it]."[23]

Case Scenario

The New York Times first began to experiment with a digital strategy in 1996. However, it was not until November 12, 2012, when Ben Thompson joined as CEO that the Times's digital strategy took off. Between 2012 and 2019, the Times's digital revenue grew to $800 million as the number of digital subscribers increased at a nearly 27% compound annual rate from 668,000 in the fourth quarter of 2012[24] to 3.5 million in the fourth quarter of 2019.[25] Moreover, between November 12, 2012, and February 21, 2020, shares of The New York Times soared 361% from $8.50 to $39.21. Thompson realized when he joined the Times that it would be difficult to change its strategy and culture. As he said, "The majority opinion of my friends [was] don't touch it with a barge pole. It is a block of concrete. You will *never move it. It's so set in its ways." Thompson concluded that the Times would not survive unless he succeeded at changing its strategy and culture. To that end, he adopted what he called a value-based leadership approach. "Once you convince people that you really believe in the fundamentals of the product and the values, then you earn permission to start talking about those things where you do need to make changes. The trick is not to try and come up with a strategy and impose it on an organization. The trick is to encourage and cajole and help the organization come up with its strategy ... and so because they come up with it, it is their strategy. They own it." One element of the strategy was to transform the Times's morning routine. Before 2012, at 7:00 a.m. the only people in the newsroom were vacuuming the carpets. But when Thompson realized that that 7:00 a.m. "was the peak time for smartphone consumption," he made sure that the newsroom was in full swing at that time to meet that demand.*[26]

The digital subscription approach that Thompson inherited was the third Times experiment aimed at generating new revenues by charging users to access its content online. The first, in 1996, required overseas users to pay $35/month to access its site. By 1998, the Times had abandoned this effort because it wanted to take advantage of faster overseas Internet growth. Times executives concluded that a no-fee business model would attract more international subscribers which would in turn accelerate the growth in its international web advertising revenue. In September 2005, the Times introduced TimesSelect – which gave readers free access everything on the site except for op-ed columns by the likes of Thomas Friedman, Nicholas Kristof, and Paul Krugman – for which readers would pay $49.95 a year to read online. By 2007, TimesSelect had attracted 227,000 paid subscribers. Yet the rise of social media and high-quality blogs generated considerable criticism of TimesSelect. That September, the Times terminated TimesSelect. Nearly four years later, after studying its previous attempts and the successes and failures of other newspapers, the Times tried again – introducing a new paywall in March 2011. After considering several pricing options, Times management opted for a device-specific and metered system that allowed users to read 20 articles a month without paying. The pricing for digital access was put into three tiers depending on the device used to access content – and by the end of 2011, digital subscribers were paying about $4.00/week. In February 2012, the Times reported 390,000 paid subscribers which Chairman Arthur Sulzberger Jr. said represented "significant strides" toward building a "new robust consumer revenue stream, while maintaining its significant digital advertising business."[27]

Under Thompson's leadership, the third paywall helped the Times surpass its goals for digital revenue. Thompson had aimed for the Times to earn $800 million in digital revenue by 2020, and in 2019, the Times surpassed that goal a year ahead of schedule. More specifically, in the final three months of 2019, the Times generated $800.8 million in digital revenue, 52% of which, or $420 million, came from news subscribers and the balance from advertising. The Times's subscriber count totaled nearly 5.3 million – 3.5 million of which were digital subscribers – and the company expected to reach 10 million total subscribers by 2025. Digital news *subscribers rose a whopping 30% in the quarter. The bad news was that digital advertising revenue fell from the previous year due to an unusually strong fourth quarter in the previous year. In forecasting 2020 results, Thompson expected digital subscription revenue to account for most of the digital revenue growth – abetted by the first price increase, to $17 from $15 every four weeks – since the Times launched the latest paywall in 2011.[28]*

What was behind its rapid growth in digital subscribers? In a nutshell, the growth came from innovative marketing and excellent digital content. During 2019, the Times added over a million new digital subscribers resulting from a new marketing approach based on speed and machine learning. Times marketing technology ran dozens of parallel tests simultaneously – identifying the most successful tactics for boosting the number of new subscriptions. The Times planned to use this technology to keep from losing subscribers as it raised prices in 2020. More specifically, the technology would gauge customer price sensitivity and set prices as high as possible before observing an increase in cancellations. By requiring people to register to read content, the Times obtained "millions" of email addresses in 2019 which boosted its marketing activity. The Times ended 2019 with a record number of journalists – 1,600[29] – many of whom produced high-quality digital reporting. The University of Colorado's Plunkett was impressed. As he said, "Back in the day, many news sites looked and performed terribly. The Times showed the world how to have a constantly updating site that is beautiful and powerful. They've figured out how to make their biggest stories really pop visually." He continued, "An example is a special report called 'The Case of Jane Doe Ponytail.' In print, it was given a standalone section with beautiful photography and layout. But look at it online! The visuals are animated, hypnotic, and really cool. I read the story first in print. I even took the print section to my class when we discussed the story. I wanted our students to see the difference. My point was that it was the first time I liked an online presentation of a big, in-depth piece more than the print version."[30]

The pandemic had a mixed effect on the Times. Its digital subscriptions hit a record – yet advertising dropped. In early March 2020, The New York Times' president and CEO, Mark Thompson, anticipated a 10% decrease in digital ad revenue in the first quarter. The actual result – reported in May 2020 – was a roughly 8% digital advertising decline, coupled with a 20.9% plunge in print advertising, resulting in a 15.2% decline in ad revenue for the quarter. The figure is just shy of 8%, but print advertising was down 20.9% in Q1, leaving a year-over-year net ad revenue decrease of 15.2%. Thanks to other sources of revenue – subscriptions and other, which rose 5.4% and 20.6%, respectively – the Times's total revenue grew 1%. The Times' coverage of the pandemic drew in 587,000 net new digital subscriptions – resulting in more than 4 million digital-only news subscriptions, more than 5 million digital-only subscriptions to specialty products (the crossword, NYT Cooking, and audio), and more than 6 million total digital and print subscribers. Thompson concluded that the Times's subscription revenue and strong balance sheet would enable the company to invest in its digital growth strategy and remain "financially sound through the pandemic."[31]

Case Analysis

The growing success of the *Times*'s digital business under Thompson revealed two fundamental truths about an effective *Follow the Leader* mindset. First, as we saw in the cases of Target and Best Buy, it almost always takes an outsider to envision a new strategy and change the company's culture and operating processes to achieve ambitious growth goals. Simply bringing in an outsider does not guarantee success – for that the outsider must have the right idea for the strategy and possess the organizational skills required to overcome the natural resistance to taking orders from an outsider. This leads to the second critical element – the strategy must be right. In the case of Thompson, the right strategy was to build on the *Times*'s biggest competitive advantage: its journalists and the industry-leading reporting they produced. Thompson bet that asking readers to subscribe to digital content would generate more revenue growth than would investing in a digital advertising service able to surpass those of Google or Facebook. Thompson's digital strategy did not so much follow these leaders as it built a stronger position in a market in which the *Times* could survive even as these two digital advertising giants continued to prevail.

Failure: *The Denver Post* Surrenders to Hedge Fund After Borrowing Too Much

Introduction

Although Buffett long admired the profit potential of local newspapers, there were many cities that lacked enough subscribers and advertisers to support the costs of operating two newspapers. For such communities, the idea that outside owners could salvage these money-bleeding newspapers was often irresistible. The lousy economics of these local newspapers always outsmarted the excessive hubris of the outside owners. These painful lessons were reinforced through the challenges of borrowing too much money, an economic downturn, bankruptcy, and newsroom cost cuts that eroded the value of the newspaper's brand. If on top of that you added the industry-wide erosion of advertising and subscription revenue caused by the rapid rise of Google and Facebook, you got the sorry tale of *The Denver Post*. While the *Post* did well in the early 2000s, the Great Recession sent its parent company into bankruptcy, and by 2020 it survived as a shadow of its former self. It is not right to say that *The Denver Post* had its head in the sand – just that it spent too much of its recent history struggling to catch up with trends and almost never succeeding.

Case Scenario

Between 1980 and 2011, The Denver Post had three different owners preceded by a colorful 85-year history. It was founded by Frederick G. Bonfils and Harry Tammen in 1895. Until 1972, it was run by Helen G. Bonfils, Bonfils' younger daughter. Known as "Miss Helen" to the employees, she spent more than three decades fighting to keep the Post under local ownership until her death at age 82. Both Bonfils and Tammen once were wounded by an attorney following a dispute over a campaign to get Alferd Packer, a miner accused of cannibalism, pardoned from the state prison. The attorney claimed he shot the pair after he was physically kicked out of their office. The Helen G. Bonfils and the Frederick G. Bonfils Foundations owned about 90% of the stock of the Post with The Denver Post Employees Stock Trust owning most of the remaining 10%. In the late 1970s, the Post suffered financial problems. So, when Times Mirror approached the Post trustees about an acquisition, the editorial staff was pleased. Earlier in 1980, 160 employee-shareholders signed a petition requesting an open meeting with trustees of the employee's stock trust to raise questions about a sale. That October, Times Mirror announced a $95 million deal to acquire the Post with an initial payment of $25 million, $55 million more at the end of 1990, and an additional $15 million in 2000.[32]

Sadly, for those Post shareholders, the Times Mirror sold its shares before that second payment. After investing $45 million in a new printing plant, the Post enjoyed a Sunday circulation lead over its rival the Rocky Mountain News but lagged the News in daily circulation. So, in September 1987, Times Mirror accepted a $95 million offer to sell the Post to publicly traded Media General run by a legendary Texas entrepreneur, William Dean Singleton. Media General put up $25 million in cash and took back a note and warrant that gave the company the right to buy 40% of The Denver Post. Times Mirror retained ownership of the Post's downtown land and buildings valued at about $20 million – leasing them back to the Post for five years.[33] *As Singleton said, "For a public company to own a newspaper that was losing money was not acceptable on Wall Street. Revenues had slumped due to the oil and gas downturn and the closure of Denver Dry Goods Co., a key advertiser. Management slashed costs with employee buyouts, deepening the $15 million loss the paper suffered in 1987." The Post was the 29th daily acquired by Singleton who was a mere 36 at the time. Although the Post trailed the News by 146,000 in daily circulation, it enjoyed a 30,000-reader lead over the News on Sunday. By cutting costs, Singleton turned what would have been an $8 million loss in 1988 into $28,000 profit. In 1989, the profit kept rising to $1.8 million; it hit $5 million in 1991 and peaked at $44 million in 1997 when the Post surpassed the News in daily circulation. The Post increased its circulation by publishing more local stories and becoming more involved with the local community through sports team partnerships and other local programs. The Post also tried to convert Sunday subscribers into full-week customers. The News counterpunched by cutting its subscription price to a penny a day. A year later the Post matched the price, but the News cut its price* *to a third of a cent per day. In 2000, the year the News lost $25 million, the Post and the News formed a joint operating agreement in which News owner E. W. Scripps paid MediaNews $60 million.*[34]

But that deal marked the beginning of the end for the Post because Singleton launched a debt-fueled spending spree. Since neither paper was in a building that could accommodate the other's staff, the partnership built a new, 11-story headquarters just north of Denver's Civic Center park and upgraded the printing presses. The newsroom staff increased from 187 at the Post to 310 combined. MediaNews invested $255 million in capital, and in 2006, it spent $1 billion to acquire papers in northern California and elsewhere. When the Great Recession hit, home and car sales plunged. What is more, classified ads had moved online, and national advertisers began to bypass local newspapers. By 2008, Scripps and MediaNews concluded that the News had to close – leaving the Post as the sole local Denver newspaper. In 2010, MediaNews filed a prepackaged bankruptcy – swapping equity to settle the claims of its bankers and most bondholders. Singleton expected that MediaNews's stock would rise from $5 to $15 a share over three years. Three months later, Manhattan hedge fund Alden Global Capital offered between $15 and $25 a share for MediaNews stock. In November 2011, Singleton stepped down as CEO of MediaNews Group but continued as chairman and as publisher of The Denver Post and The Salt Lake Tribune. Two years later he retired as chairman and publisher.[35]

The Alden era was difficult for the Post's newsroom. In 2018, the Post made national headlines for published editorials that called out Alden's cost-cutting tactics. Another painful downsizing – in April 2018, a 30% cut in newsroom staff from 100 to 70 journalists – prompted Plunkett, then-editorial page editor at the Post, to publish a series of editorials criticizing Alden. The ensuing publicity highlighted Alden's strategy of buying distressed newspapers at a low price, cutting newsroom and other fixed costs, and raising the profit margins from print advertising. These editorials prompted the Post and Plunkett to part ways.[36] *Alden had other tactics to profit from the Post deal. When an Alden-holding company, Digital First, acquired the Post, it sold the paper's printing plant – where its offices were moved – to an Alden subsidiary, Twenty Lake Holdings, meaning the Alden-controlled newspaper became a tenant of an Alden-controlled landlord.*[37] *By February 2020, the job cuts had ended, according to editor Lee Ann Colacioppo who boasted of the newsroom's eagerness to do "important, relevant work."*[38]

Case Analysis

The Denver Post suffered through many seasons of insolvency during its long history. In 1979, with the local economy weakened by an oil bust and the loss of a major advertiser, the *Post* sold out to Times Mirror. After investing $45 million in a new printing plant, the Post was still losing money, so the *Times Mirror* sold it to Singleton's *MediaNews* in 1987. While Singleton made some savvy moves – such as improving the *Post's* local coverage and sustaining a lead in the Sunday paper war with *Rocky Mountain News* – his decision to borrow money to build a pricey headquarters building for the merged *Post* and *News* and make $1 billion worth of acquisitions sent the company into bankruptcy in 2010. After Alden Global Capital took over, asset stripping and layoffs followed. And with Google and Facebook having stripped away the industry's formerly profitable print advertising business, the *Post* survived as a shadow of its former self.

Newspaper Industry Case Study Takeaways

The takeaways from these case studies have varying implications depending on where you sit.

Incumbent Executives

- **Do:** Based on *The New York Times* case, newspaper executives may sustain competitive advantage by
    - Hiring reporters who can create uniquely valuable content for which subscribers are willing to pay
    - Seeking out owners who are committed to investing in the mission of a newspaper as a guardian of democratic ideals
- **Do not:** Based on all the cases, newspaper executives should avoid self-destructive tactics such as
    - Borrowing to acquire other newspapers and expect to achieve profitability by cutting costs.
    - Attempting to make up for the decline in print advertising revenue through much more price-competitive digital advertising.
    - Cutting costs and expecting revenues to rise. As newspapers reduce reporting staff, the quality of the newspaper will decline, and print subscriber cancellations will accelerate – thus deepening operating losses.

Incumbent Employees

- **Do:** Based on *The New York Times* case, newspaper employees should seek employment at newspapers that are boosting the number of newsroom employees. Sadly, due to the large number of layoffs of experienced journalists, the competition for such positions is likely to be very stiff.

- **Do not:** Based on *The Denver Post* case, reporters who work for newspapers owned by private equity or hedge funds should anticipate that they could be dismissed from their positions and, therefore, they should seek employment with more financially stable firms – such as public relations firms or within the media organizations of established companies.

Startup CEOs

- **Do:** Based on *The New York Times* case, there may be opportunities for startups to work with established newspapers to help them develop much higher-quality digital media that is more compelling than traditional print presentations.
- **Do not:** Based on the Google case, Startup CEOs should avoid trying to compete in search or advertising platforms because they are unlikely to prevail in the battle for searchers or advertisers seeking to reach them. Moreover, founders should not attempt to start a news website unless it offers unique content that is highly in demand.

Business Students

- **Do:** Business students should seek employment at Google due to the strength of its people, its alumni network, and the industry knowledge they will gain from working there.
- **Do not:** Based on all the cases, business students should not seek employment in the newspaper industry unless they are comfortable struggling to hold down a job.

Do You Have the Strategic Mindset of a Newspaper Industry Winner?

If you answer in the affirmative to these questions, you have a winning strategic mindset. If not, you must decide whether to change your mindset, strategy, and execution or find a job that better suits your strengths and interests:

- Does your newspaper know specifically what stories are most compelling to its readers?
- Are you hiring and developing reporters and columnists who can deliver such content in ways the readers prefer to alternative providers?

- Can you deliver such stories and other content in formats that readers prefer?
- Are readers willing to pay a high enough price for that content to make your newspaper sustainable?
- Can your newspaper provider advertising and other content that is profitable to deliver and that preserves the integrity of the newspaper's editorial content?

Conclusion

The newspaper industry is shrinking and becoming less profitable. The decline of the newspaper industry threatens one of the key underpinnings of democracy. The biggest threat to the newspaper industry resulted from the success of *Create the Future* companies such as Google and Facebook at building systems that capture and hold readers' attention more effectively than newspapers did. As readers increasingly went to search engines and social networks, advertisers followed them. Google and Facebook also created advertising platforms that provide advertisers with measurable return on marketing budgets – far superior to print advertising whose benefit is virtually impossible to measure. These two companies have siphoned marketing budgets from newspapers, and only a few *Follow the Leader* companies – such as *The New York Times* and *The Wall Street Journal* – have built the ability to produce world-beating journalism for which readers are willing to pay. Most other newspapers more or less have operated with their *Heads in the Sand* and have lost their independence to private equity and hedge fund investors which are dedicated to maximizing the cash flow harvest from the declining newspaper industry for as long as it lasts. Chapter 5 will examine how these three mindsets play out for the grocery industry.

CHAPTER

5

Groceries

The grocery industry was large, slowly growing, and barely profitable. Yet because consumers needed to purchase groceries at least every week, the industry was full of creative competitors. Rivals vied for grocery shoppers because of the potential to profit from regularly supplementing sales of groceries with other products and services. Such cross-selling was aimed at strengthening their bonds with customers and thereby boosting their lifetime value. The grocery industry's dynamism offered excellent examples of how important a CEO's strategic mindset is to achieve long-term success. Lessons for leaders include

- **Know how well your strengths match the requirements of success in the industry:** In previous chapters we saw that superior information systems can make the difference between success and failure. In the grocery industry, physical world strengths are more important because consumers like to shop in stores to make sure that they are putting the best items in their baskets. Therefore, a company that excels at information technology innovation but lacks the ability to purchase, warehouse, and retail groceries at scale will be at a competitive disadvantage. Leaders of such companies must have the intellectual humility to recognize that they will not be successful in the industry unless they can bolster those weaknesses.

P. S. Cohan, *Goliath Strikes Back*, https://doi.org/10.1007/978-1-4842-6519-2_5

- **Partner with others who excel in critical activities in which you are weak:** Once such executives realize that they lack enough strength in those critical activities, they must close the capability gap. To do that effectively, leaders will need to acquire, partner, or create them internally. Moreover, leaders who can reinvent their companies must master new management skills – such as attracting and motivating talent in fields which are new to the leaders. Leaders can only achieve this if they have a desire and ability to learn new concepts and skills.
- **Choose your successor wisely:** Leaders who build successful companies must choose successors with a *Create the Future* or *Follow the Leader* mindset. As we will see in the following A&P case, leaders who turn their company into a dominant player risk endangering its future if they appoint a loyalist who lacks creative spark to succeed them. To sustain industry dominance, successful founders must appoint successors with a demonstrated knack for successful corporate reinvention.

These implications emerge from examining the surprising level of creativity in what was a slowly growing, barely profitable industry fraught with fragmentation and price competition and slightly bolstered by consolidation. Between 2014 and 2019, the industry eked out a 1.3% annual increase to $666.5 billion and was expected to grow slightly more quickly – up 1.6% – to $720 billion between 2019 and 2024. The average grocer's profit increased slightly between 2014 and 2019, from 1.4% to 1.7%, and was expected to remain stable through 2024. While consumer incomes rose through 2019, intense rivalry in this fragmented industry – in which the top three firms controlled a mere 31% of the market – fueled price competition. This competition led to some consolidation. The number of grocery chains fell to 41,556 at an average 0.2% annual rate in the five years ending 2019. Despite these difficulties, some competitors were growing much faster than the industry by appealing to specific demographic segments such as millennials and baby boomers with unique store formats. Underlying the intense rivalry were the rising popularity of so-called alternative retailers who grew quickly to the detriment of larger incumbents. Costco and Walmart attracted consumers seeking lower prices and greater convenience. Mass merchandisers used their relatively high purchase volumes to negotiate discounts which they passed on to consumers as lower prices. Some consumers opted for limited assortment and fresh format stores such as Aldi and Trader Joe's that provided mostly lower-priced store-brand products. Trader Joe's enjoyed the highest sales per square foot in the industry, and over 80% of its goods were private-label and free of

GMOs, artificial coloring, trans fat, and high-fructose corn syrup. Many large national grocery chains responded to this threat by offering discounts and promotions to encourage more consumers to visit and remain loyal to their stores. Some national chains offset slower organic growth by acquiring rivals – however, the high prices paid for such acquisitions kept a lid on their profitability.[1]

Much of the innovation in the grocery industry was aimed at the United States' largest generation – millennials. Millennials were both health conscious and value driven. 42% of millennial grocery shoppers found private-label foods more innovative than branded products, and about 70% believed that the quality of private-label products had increased. Larger operators adapted to the success that Trader Joe's and Aldi enjoyed at maintaining millennials as loyal customers. Whole Foods announced plans to open small private-label stores targeted at millennials. Ahold, a Netherlands-based operator with storefronts in New England and the Mid-Atlantic, introduced similar stores branded bfresh. By 2024, more such brands were expected to enter the market. Other traditional supermarkets opted instead to add new services – such as home grocery delivery, movie rental services, ATMs, dining areas, and beer and wine bars – to their existing stores.[2] Meanwhile, Trader Joe's and Aldi were among the lower-priced health food retailers that threatened specialty grocers which had pioneered natural food retailing. By March 2020, regional chains Earth Fare, Lucky's Market, and Fairway Market had filed for bankruptcy. Since March 2018, shares of Farmers Market and Natural Grocers by Vitamin Cottage had declined about 30% and nearly 50%, respectively. Whole Foods's ability to offer rapid delivery via Amazon was another factor that won over many former customers of such natural food retailers. For example, Green Aisle Grocery closed its two Philadelphia stores in January 2020 after sales decreased 30% over the previous two years. Coowner Andrew Erace said, "I can't compete with that. I don't have the technology to implement for our small shops."[3] Finally, by 2024 more grocers with greater resources were expected to compete with Amazon and meal-kit service Blue Apron by offering online ordering coupled with same-day in-store grocery pickup or delivery to the home.[4]

Because grocers and supermarkets were considered essential businesses – remained open throughout the pandemic – Covid-19 was not expected to reduce industry revenues. IBISWorld expected sluggish growth for the industry in 2020 for two reasons: consumers were likely to visit supermarkets and grocery stores less frequently to prevent the spread of Covid-19 and per capita disposable income was forecast to fall. As a result, demand for higher-quality, more expensive products was expected to decline – thus crimping industry profitability.[5]

Strategic Mindsets of Grocery Industry Winners and Losers

The grocery industry is large and thinly profitable – yet compared to newspapers, it is a hotbed of innovation. Interestingly, unlike many industries analyzed in this book, groceries are relatively immune to being replaced by an app. While apps can make it easier to place orders, most of the value created for consumers results from excellence in fulfilling orders. Therefore, it may be easier for grocery chains – with excellent supplier ties and well-located warehouses, trucking networks, and retail stores – to adopt to technological innovations than it is for tech innovators to beef up their supply chains enough to take on those leading grocery chains. Simply put, in the grocery industry, innovative technology is not as much of a source of competitive advantage as operating a supply chain that provides low-priced groceries, delivered at a time and place of the customer's choosing.

Grocery Industry Startup and Incumbent Success and Failure Case Studies

In the following case studies explored, we will examine how the three strategic mindsets have played out in the grocery industry:

- **Executives with a *Create the Future* mindset were winners:** Executives who were determined to create the future of the grocery industry – specifically, Amazon's CEO Jeff Bezos – tried many different experiments with local online ordering and delivery, various retail store formats, and the acquisition of Whole Foods. In 2020, after 13 years of trying to reinvent the grocery industry, Amazon was barely halfway to its 2025 target of $30 billion in grocery revenue. Nevertheless, Bezos was undeterred–realizing that if his persistent experimentation paid off, Amazon would be able to boost the predictability of its revenues since consumers would always need groceries about once a week.
- **Companies with a *Follow the Leader* mindset had the potential to strengthen their market position by adapting Amazon's innovations:** In exploring the growth of its industry-leading grocery business, it became clear that Walmart's focus on large-scale purchasing, delivery, and warehousing of good-quality groceries at a low price in convenient retail locations enabled it to build a leading competitive position. Walmart strengths proved

an excellent platform from which the company could adopt some of Amazon's online ordering innovations.

- ***Head in the Sand* leaders ultimately presided over the bankruptcy of their companies:** The A&P case explored in this chapter exemplifies the importance of strategic mindset to a company's success or failure. George Hartford, who started A&P, sold tea in New York City. His sons John and George reinvented A&P four times between the early 1900s and 1950s – during which time A&P dominated the grocery market with nearly 16,000 stores. When they handed the reins over to a longtime loyalist, they charged him with maximizing A&P's dividends to fund a foundation they created. During the decades that followed, A&P lost touch with the changing needs of customers and successful strategies of innovative upstarts. Ultimately, A&P was acquired in 1979, filed for bankruptcy in 2010, emerged in 2012, and failed for good in 2015. Over its 156-year history, A&P benefited from leaders with a *Create the Future* mindset and stumbled and collapsed from a *Head in the Sand* one.

Success: Amazon Experiments, Innovates, and Acquires Its Way into Groceries

Introduction

Amazon spent over a decade trying to invent a new way for consumers to purchase and take delivery of groceries. Although Amazon began in 2007 to explore ways to take grocery orders online and deliver them to consumers' homes, dubbed Amazon Fresh, its experiments did not generate meaningful market share. With Amazon's ambitions unfulfilled, in June 2017 the company paid $13.7 billion to acquire Whole Foods Market – giving Amazon 2.6% of the grocery industry and over 460 stores nationwide.[6] In addition, by 2020 Amazon was developing retail grocery stores that enabled consumers to buy with a mobile device rather than paying the cashier. Although Amazon had yet to create a uniquely compelling future for the grocery industry, it remained relentless in its pursuit of innovations that would bring that vision closer to reality.

Case Scenario

After a decade of experiments such as Amazon Fresh, its online grocery ordering and delivery service offered in various cities, Amazon encountered numerous obstacles. Amazon concluded that a physical store was an essential ingredient for achieving Bezos's big ambitions. The grocery industry was compelling to Amazon *and incumbent mass merchandisers because it was large and a source of ongoing customer purchases. Walmart and Target saw groceries as an essential way to attract more customers and encourage existing customers to boost the amount and frequency of their purchases. Yet the path to online grocery success was paved with at least one spectacular failure: Webvan – an online grocer that launched in June 1999 – went public a few months later at a $7.9 billion valuation, never made a profit, and filed for bankruptcy in 2001 tossing 2,000 employees out of their jobs.[7] Webvan failed due to many management mistakes – among the most significant was investing heavily to build a national network of warehouses and trucks before proving that online grocery delivery could work locally. In establishing Amazon Fresh, former Amazon and Webvan executives said that Bezos drew three big lessons from Webvan's demise: "expand slowly, limit delivery to areas with a high concentration of potential customers, and focus relentlessly on warehouse efficiency."[8] Bezos explained his mindset for creating new businesses in a television interview with Charlie Rose. "We like to pioneer; we like to explore. Every new business that we have ever invested in has taken years…if you're going to invent new things ... you've got to be willing to endure a lot of criticism." Former Amazon executive John Rossman – who ran its third-party seller business, Amazon Marketplace – described how Amazon would combine what it learned from its various grocery initiatives into a grocery store of the future. Rossman said, "Once they get the technology and operations really pressure-tested and proven, then they'll figure out how to roll it over. It will take a long time and it will feel like Amazon is crawling. It won't be like a light switch flipped on and off."[9] Amazon's set ambitious goals in the grocery industry. By 2017, Amazon's goal was to become one of the five largest grocery retailers by 2025. Cowen estimated that to achieve that goal, Amazon's grocery industry revenues would need to exceed $30 billion – more than three times the $8.7 billion Amazon generated in 2016 through Amazon Fresh and all its other food and drink sales.[10]*

Amazon's first experiment with online grocery delivery began in August 2007. Amazon Fresh began operating in Mercer Island, Washington – adjusting its operations over six years (trying a free loyalty program called Big Radish and testing free or discounted delivery based on a customer's spending volume). In 2013, Fresh expanded to Los Angeles and San Francisco. Amazon encountered significant operational problems with Fresh. At its Seattle fulfillment center, Amazon wasted nearly a third of the bananas it purchased because Fresh only sold the fruit in bunches of five. Workers discarded any bunches of three or four and tore off and threw out the extra banana on a bunch of six, according to a 2015 research paper by an MIT student.[11] Worse, poorly trained employees often stood around with no assigned work, disappointed customers frequently returned moldy strawberries, and Amazon's inspectors believed that top executives were indifferent to the quality of the food provided.[12] Despite the challenges, Fresh continued to expand to new markets in the United States and in 2017 launched in Tokyo. CFO Brian Olsavsky said in an October 2016 analyst conference call that although customers saw it as "a very attractive service," Fresh's costs were too high, and it was unprofitable.[13]

Despite efforts to expand the category, by 2016 only 4.5% of shoppers frequently purchased groceries online – one possible reason was that people enjoyed visiting grocery stores more than taking delivery at home.[14]

Amazon concluded that it would need to add retail stores to achieve its ambitious goals for the grocery industry. Initially, Amazon experimented with opening its own retail stores and ultimately decided to supplement these efforts by acquiring Whole Foods. In 2016, Amazon acquired a supply chain software firm. All this experimentation resulted in a confusing array of options for consumers. By 2017, Amazon Fresh was available in about 20 US cities for $14.99 a month; Amazon Pantry charged shoppers $5.99 to deliver boxes of nonperishables – such as crackers, cookies, chips, and coffee. Amazon's drop-off service, Prime Now, offered items from local grocers in some cities, but no major chains. Its stick-on Dash Buttons enabled consumers to order some groceries, but not fresh food – with a finger tap. And Amazon's Subscribe & Save offered discounts to Amazon customers who signed up for periodic delivery of items available in grocery stores such as laundry detergent, toothpaste, diapers, and paper towels. In 2017, Amazon restructured its grocery teams to narrow their focus and set clear priorities. Amazon also planned to open as many as 2,000 stores along the lines of three bricks and mortar grocery formats in Seattle – convenience stores called Amazon Go, drive-in grocery kiosks, and a hybrid supermarket that mixed online and in-store shopping benefits. Amazon Go was full of technological innovation. Cameras and sensors monitored shoppers who scanned their smartphones when they entered the store. Once checked in they could take sandwiches, yogurt, drinks, and snacks and pay for them without a checkout kiosk. Products were embedded with tracking devices that paired with customers' phones to charge their accounts. Weight-sensitive shelves told Amazon when to restock. In 2016, Amazon executives concluded that these options might not be enough. Instead they considered opening up Trader Joe's sized grocery stories that would offer consumers items such as milk, eggs, and produce with other items – such as paper towels, cereal, canned goods, and dish detergent – stocked in an on-site warehouse where they could be easily packed and delivered to shoppers at the location.[15] *By February 2020, Amazon operated 25 Go stores in Seattle, New York, Chicago, and San Francisco, which ranged in size from about 450 square feet to 2,300 square feet.*[16]

By 2019, Amazon's acquisition of Whole Foods gave Amazon 2.6% of the grocery market. Whole Foods operated over 500 locations in the United States, Canada, and the United Kingdom – supplementing branded products with Whole Foods private-label brands, such as 365 Everyday Value and Wellshire Farms. Whole Foods stores were equipped with hot food bars, juice stations, and other amenities. Amazon's ownership of Whole Foods resulted in a decrease in Whole Foods' prices – for example, cutting the price of Atlantic salmon from $12.99 to $9.99 a pound, extending Whole Foods discounts to Amazon Prime members, and making products available online.[17] *By April 2019, Amazon had instituted a third round of price cuts at Whole Foods – slashing prices 20% on hundreds of items. For the year ending August 2019, prices at Whole Foods dropped by 2.5%. These price cuts reduced the*

Whole Foods premium over regional supermarket chains such as Kroger from 20% before Amazon acquired the grocer to a range of 12% to 13%.[18] *By November 2019, Amazon was planning in 2020 to launch yet another grocery store concept – a Woodland Hills, Calif. store targeting a wider customer base eager to purchase brand-name sodas, cereals, and sweets paying through conventional checkout lines rather than that natural foods offered to more upscale customers by Whole Foods's.*[19] *In 2019, Amazon's grocery revenue was estimated at $17.2 billion.*[20]

Covid-19 increased demand for ordering grocery items on Amazon's website; however, Amazon lost ground to Walmart's online grocery order and store pickup service since its 4,700 stores vastly outnumbered Whole Foods's roughly 500. Sucharita Kodali, a retail and ecommerce analyst with research firm Forrester, pointed out that only 150 of Whole Foods stores were offering in-store pickup while 3,200 Walmart stores offered the popular service. Customers who shop in Walmart's stores were more likely to buy from the company online. Curbside pickup enabled customers to book a time slot and collect their groceries easily and with little interaction. While demand for Amazon's own grocery business soared during state lockdowns, it struggled to keep up with customer demand, delayed shipments on nonessential items and ran out of products that customers wanted. Amazon was at a disadvantage to Walmart which had strong relationships with all the major suppliers of consumer-packaged goods, according to Kodali.[21]

Case Analysis

Amazon's original name was Relentless.com. This seems particularly apt in considering the 13-year marathon in which Amazon has tried many different approaches to gaining market share in the grocery industry. Its innovations included online ordering with local delivery, cashier-less stores, and many others. Yet by March 2020, the move that enabled Amazon to gain the most market share was its 2017 acquisition of Whole Foods. Despite having a long way to go to achieve its goal of $30 billion in grocery revenue by 2025, Amazon's pursuit of grocery industry market share showed no signs of slowing down. One big challenge facing Amazon was its competitive disadvantage to Walmart in servicing consumers seeking to order online and take delivery at a store.

Success: Walmart Builds a Huge Grocery Chain and Carefully Adds Delivery

Introduction

Walmart's founder Sam Walton was as inspiring an entrepreneur in his day as Jeff Bezos was in 2020. Walton imbued his company with the idea that the customer was the boss. He hired and promoted people who took the initiative to develop new ways to serve those customers well. Walmart pushed suppliers to reduce prices every year in exchange for enormous purchases of their products. And Walmart used technology to help save money in logistics and operations – passing the lower costs to consumers in the form of lower prices – which attracted more customers and kept them loyal. Walmart applied this philosophy to the grocery industry – which it entered in 1987. Yet after Walton departed as CEO, Walmart lost some of its innovative edge – and stumbled to compete effectively in the world of ecommerce which Amazon pioneered. Nevertheless, by 2020 Walmart enjoyed a significant share of the grocery industry and had established a popular service enabling consumers to order online and pick up at the store or take delivery at home.

Case Scenario

Walmart – founded by Sam Walton in 1962 – began selling groceries in 1987, and by 2019, it was the United States' largest grocer – with estimated 2019 grocery revenue of $191 billion (56% of its 2019 US revenue of $341 billion). In the quarter ending October 2019, Walmart generated considerable grocery revenue online. Demand for groceries propelled its ecommerce sales 41% as shoppers picked up groceries at 3,100 US stores or had them delivered to their houses from 1,400 stores. By 2019, most of Walmart's grocery revenue came from its Sam's Club, supercenter stores. Walmart's delivery network helped it outpace peers such as Amazon, Kroger, Costco, and Aldi.[22] *Walmart also generated significant grocery revenue through its Neighborhood Markets, a chain of smaller grocery stores launched in 1998 which included pharmacies, liquor stores, delis, bakeries, and photo shops. By 2019, Walmart operated 800 locations across 36 states and Washington, DC.*[23] *Walmart first began selling groceries in its Hypermart USA stores, opened in 1987, which combined a grocery store, a merchandise market, restaurants, and video rental stores. Although the hypermarts expanded rapidly across the United States, it was not until 1988 that they included a fully stocked grocery. Walmart enjoyed greater success with its supercenters – a combination discount outlet and fully stocked grocer – which began operating in 1988 and eventually replaced hypermarkets. As mentioned earlier, a decade later Walmart launched the Neighborhood Markets. In 1993, Walmart introduced its Great Value line which by 2002 included over 100 product categories.*[24]

Walmart's move into groceries was spearheaded by Walton's successor, David Glass, who saw offering groceries to save time for consumers by enabling them to one-stop-shop. Glass exemplified how to succeed a charismatic founder – humbly lead a team that follows the founder's principles. As Glass explained in 2004, "Most people have enough ego that they want to distinguish themselves from a charismatic leader, and that's what creates the problem. I have never had much ego, and I am not worried about things like that. I am more interested in the satisfaction that we are doing the right things and we are getting it done and being a part of it. I like being part of a winning team. I do not have to be the winning team. [When I joined Walmart in 1976] the company was completely different from any I had been around. Mostly because of Sam and the charisma and the drive he had. He had this desire to improve that I have not seen. I can count on one hand the people I have known who got up every morning and really tried to improve something–either in their business or in their lives. Sam worked at it seven days a week. The company was more intense than any I had been around. We had to be. We were 4%, 5% the size of Kmart. Sam was doing some things, even when I came, that were foreign to me. He shared total financial information with everyone in every store, in every community. Sam felt we were all partners, and he wanted to share everything. And he was absolutely right. He believed that everyone should be an entrepreneur. If you ran the toy department in a store in Harrison, Ark., you would have all your financial information. So, you are just like the toy entrepreneur of Harrison: You know what your sales are, what your margins are, what your inventory is. And then we had another philosophy where we had grass-roots meetings in every store. And there was an absolute belief that the best ideas ever at Wal-Mart came from the bottom up. Ideas would come up from those meetings and be implemented companywide. The door greeter, for example, was the idea of an hourly associate in Louisiana."[25]

Walmart was criticized for entering the low-margin grocery business and for its various failed experiments. Walmart's logic for entering the grocery industry sprang from a fundamental principle of its founder: customer is boss. As Walmart CEO Doug McMillon explained, "Customers…want to save time and they want to save money. And the broad assortment, when you put food next to general merchandise, you ended up picking up an even bigger basket. And they designed the supercenter with pharmacy and food service and all these components, it just made it a great place to shop. You can get good value, you can get quality merchandise, it was in stock, people were friendly, and you had that breadth of assortment…Very few of our competitors have any kind of grocery capability like we do." To order online and enable customers to pick up at the store, Walmart enjoyed a significant advantage over rivals like Amazon who had not developed the ability to manage the supply chain for fresh food at a large scale. As McMillon said, "Doing food, especially fresh, in an environment where you don't have store traffic is really hard because if you don't sell that fresh product, it's got to be thrown away, which is obviously wasteful and also expensive. And so now we have got this situation where these supercenters can be leveraged with a flow. Again, self-distribution, build the warehouses, have the low cost, have the reliability of supply, have experienced buyers."[26]

A dozen years after Amazon began experimenting with online ordering and delivery to the home, Walmart began testing a new delivery-to-the-home service. The service – dubbed InHome grocery delivery – charged consumers $19.95 a month to order online from Walmart and take delivery to refrigerators either in their home kitchen or garage. Shoppers purchased $49.95 smart door lock kits, and Walmart employees – with at least a year of service with the company, background checks, motor vehicle record checks, and training – delivered the goods. In October 2019, InHome was launched in Kansas City, Pittsburgh, and Vero Beach, Fla. InHome offered consumers a limited number of items – the 30,000 and 35,000 available through the Walmart grocery app. The idea for InHome was originally launched in New York with a group of ten employees in Walmart's Store No. 8 technology *incubator program. InHome was being added to its other grocery programs which included free online grocery pickup at over 2,700 locations and Delivery Unlimited – for which shoppers paid $98 annually or $12.95 monthly for unlimited grocery deliveries from 1,400 shops.[27] Customers who tried InHome kept using it. As McMillon said, "We have not had one single customer try it that doesn't keep it. I really think there will be a moment in time where you think of Walmart just as a service. The average household may have about 100 items between cleaning suppliers, paper goods, fresh and perishable foods that you just buy all the time, and we will just manage that for you. our customers are asking us [to keep sending the same one or two delivery people to their homes]. At scale, we may be able to get it down to where it is one, two, three people. But we show you on the app, like there will be a profile, Becky. Here is who she is, maybe a thumbnail. Like one of them I saw was like: Becky likes tacos, she has a dog, and she is a parent. She's a mom of three."[28]*

Walmart enjoyed a surge in demand at the beginning of the pandemic. Its quarterly sales rose 10% – including a 74% increase in ecommerce. The number of new customers trying its online grocery pickup and delivery service increased fourfold between the middle of March and early May 2020. While the number of people visiting its retail stores declined, the average transaction size rose 16.5%. To satisfy this surge in demand, Walmart incurred about $900 million in additional costs including raising warehouse wages and paying bonuses to store staff. Walmart's chief financial officer said, "It is a big advantage being an omnichannel retailer and I think that is showing right now. We had backups in our fulfillment centers too. That is something that our competitors, they can't all do it." Walmart did not experience an increase in demand for clothing and other discretionary items. However, its US sales of groceries and health-care products spiked in March and then slowed in the first half of April. Walmart focused on adding third-party sellers to Walmart.com, delivering online orders from stores and adding online grocery service to many stores. During the quarter Walmart started temporarily using about 2,500 stores to ship out online orders.[29]

Case Analysis

Walmart's grocery business is considerably larger than Amazon's. Walmart is bigger in groceries because its purchasing scale enables it to offer consumers lower prices and its larger store network gives Walmart access to more consumers who appreciate the lower grocery prices and more convenient shopping locations. Since many people enjoy visiting stores to pick out what goes into their grocery shopping cart, the industry has been more immune to the ecommerce model of shopping and purchasing online while taking delivery to the home. After all, picking the perfect tomato off the shelf is not the same as ordering one online and hoping what gets delivered is edible. While Walmart was slow to experiment with online ordering, its stores were a convenient place for consumers to take same-day delivery. And its recently introduced grocery home delivery offerings indicate that Walmart is adapting to consumer demand – which rose during the Covid-19 pandemic – for a service that Amazon pioneered.

Failure: After 156 Years, A&P Goes Bankrupt for the Second and Final Time

Introduction

CEO mindset is a powerful force that can bring a company to great success and lead to its downfall. Simply put, a *Create the Future* CEO can turn an idea into an industry-leading dynamo. And that same company's next CEO can bury his head in the sand and lead that same company to its demise. This comes to mind in considering the fate of A&P. Its founders, the Hartford brothers, built the chain of small grocery stores into the Walmart or Amazon of its day. A&P's ubiquitous stores offered goods that consumers wanted at low prices, thanks to the volume discounts it extracted from suppliers. The Hartfords retired and put in their stead a CEO whom they charged with maximizing dividends rather than keeping up with changing demographics and upstart rivals. Eventually A&P was too crippled to survive the loss of competitive edge resulting from the change in CEO mindset between its pioneering leaders and their successors.

Case Scenario

A&P launched in 1859 and until the 1950s it was a grocery industry leader. A&P was founded in 1859. By 1878, the Great Atlantic & Pacific Tea Company (A&P) – originally referred to as the Great American Tea Company – had grown to 70 stores. A&P introduced the nation's first "supermarket" – a 28,125-square-foot store in Braddock, Pennsylvania – in 1936 and, by the 1940s, operated at nearly 16,000 locations.[30] John and George Hartford, who ran A&P, developed the A&P Economy Store in 1912 – with low prices and limited selection. The store's interior was plain, it did not offer delivery or grant credit, but it made money with relatively low prices. The success of these stores convinced the Hartfords to open hundreds of new ones each year during and after World War I. In the 1920s, by which time A&P had thousands of stores, it backward integrated – operating bakeries, chocolate and pasta manufacturing, and salmon and vegetable canning. A&P became America's largest food buyer – and used its bargaining power to demand that food manufacturers and produce suppliers bypass wholesalers, offer volume discounts, and pay A&P the commission suppliers would have paid wholesalers.[31] At its peak, A&P was the largest retailer in the world operating nearly 16,000 grocery stores in 3,800 communities, along with dozens of warehouses and factories.[32]

A&P remained dominant thanks to the way that the Hartford brothers kept reinventing it. The first reinvention started soon after they took control of A&P from their father, George, in the early 1900s. The brothers turned A&P from tea shops to grocery stores that sold canned goods, cleaning products, cigarettes, and private-label products branded with "A&P" in gold letters inside a red circle. The next wave of A&P reinvention happened in 1912 when it had about 400 stores. The brothers applied Frederick Taylor's scientific management method – measuring worker's time and motion to boost productivity. John pioneered the S&P Economy Store – a single employee would staff a bare-bones store with few products, low prices, no credit, or delivery to the home. While A&P executives opposed John's idea, the A&P Economy Store spread across the United States at the rate of 10 per week – earning A&P shareholders a much higher return on investment than its larger stores. By the 1920s, the Economy Store was looking dated so the Hartfords remade A&P for the third time – acquiring suppliers such as salmon canneries, condensed milk plants, and bakeries. The new A&P combination stores – which sold meat and produce alongside packaged staples – were twice as big as the Economy Stores and more profitable. By 1929, A&P was the first retailer to top $1 billion in sales. In 1930, a new retail concept – the supermarket – was launched by A&P rivals. It was not until 1937 that A&P launched its fourth reinvention under the Hartford brothers. They wanted A&P to launch its own supermarkets – but they first needed to overcome fierce internal opposition because opening supermarkets would require the closure of combination stores and the demotion of their managers. The Hartford brothers overcame their objections by pounding the table and making clear that A&P's failure to change would result in its extinction. By 1939, A&P operated more supermarkets than all competitors combined.[33]

The Hartfords chose Ralph Burger, a man who had worked for A&P for decades, as president in 1951. He was also named head of the John A. Hartford Foundation, which controlled nearly half the company's shares after the brothers died. This was a conflict of interest: the John A. Hartford Foundation, one of the country's largest foundations at the time, needed dividends to support its medical research programs, but those generous dividends starved the company of cash to invest. The brothers selected him as their successor because they valued his loyalty. But there may not have been better internal options. All of A&P's top executives during the Hartfords' time spent their entire careers at A&P, so were not likely to be creative thinkers. Under Burger's tenure, A&P began its decline. A&P had difficulty adapting to changing consumer tastes. It was slow to follow its customers to the suburbs and declined to expand in California, the country's fastest-growing state. As other grocery chains broadened their product lines, A&P continued to sell only groceries.[34] By the late 1950s, A&P had lost its position as the low-cost retailer. It exemplified a fundamental truth: when a business stops changing, it sentences itself to death.[35]

In 1979, A&P lost its independence to West Germany's Tengelmann Group which acquired the once-venerated grocery chain. This precipitated an expansion effort that led to the acquisition of Stop & Shop stores in New Jersey, the Kohl's chain in Wisconsin, and ShopWell.[36] When Walmart began expanding into food retailing in the 1990s, it drove A&P out of many of its markets in the South and Midwest where it had once been the leading player and had become a regional grocer with high prices and dowdy stores, the sort of place your grandmother shopped. Its brands, formerly some of the most valuable consumer-product brands in the country, had entirely lost their cachet, and the A&P brand itself had become a liability. By the time of its first bankruptcy filing, in 2010, it was a shadow of its former self.[37] *Due to a series of operational and financial obstacles, including high labor costs and fast-changing trends within the grocery industry, by 2006 A&P had reduced its footprint to just over 400. In 2008, A&P acquired its largest competitor, Pathmark Stores, to continue expanding its brand portfolio and, in doing so, became the largest supermarket chain in the New York City area. A&P continued to suffer cash flow problems due to high-cost supplier contracts, bloated labor costs, and too much debt.*[38] *By the time it went bankrupt the first time, in 2010, it had long since lost its unique character. It emerged from bankruptcy in 2012, but still had nothing special to offer food shoppers.*[39]

In July 2015, A&P filed for bankruptcy for the last time. With 28,500 employees, it announced plans to close 25 stores, sell 120 to other chains, and find buyers for the other 176. A&P was battered by mass merchandisers such as Walmart, as well as dollar stores, convenience chains, and discount grocers like Aldi which won over cost-conscious consumers, while Whole Foods and others attracted more high-end customers. A&P locked itself into a cost-cutting loop in response to declining sales which kept it from hiring qualified people, purchasing sufficient inventory to meet demand, or matching rivals' heavy discounts. With liabilities of $2.3 billion and assets about $1.6 billion, A&P was unable to boost revenues and lower its costs enough to pay its bills. A&P said its high costs and declining profitability prevented it from investing as much as it planned in improvements since its 2010 bankruptcy. As a result, it was unable to offer a sufficiently compelling value proposition – including satisfying the demand for fresh, natural, and organic food – needed to attract and retain new customers.[40]

Ultimately, A&P's demise was due to its inability to adapt to a changing world. By 2020, the grocery industry was rife with experimentation. After decades of increased square footage, the average supermarket was declining as upstart grocers opened smaller stores. Market segmentation proliferated. Some retailers competed with restaurants by offering prepared food. Others installed coffee bars and eat-in restaurants. Dollar stores and pharmacies vied with supermarkets by supplying basic assortments of food, and low-cost providers appealed to mainstream consumers who had diverse and frequently changing preferences. Consumers' desire for locally grown produce and for meat from cattle raised humanely on nearby farms challenged the centralized distribution systems of traditional grocers. Grocers who decided to focus on new customers – for example, adding smaller stores to its core supercenter customers – were stymied. To make the transition work, they needed to retool their distribution network – including warehouses and inventory systems – to satisfy smaller stores' differing requirements.[41]

Case Analysis

A&P's rise and fall reinforces the critical importance of the CEO's mindset in determining a company's success or failure. A&P's greatest successes occurred under the Hartford brothers who persistently overcame internal and external challenges that sought to impede the realization of their vision to stay ahead of changing consumer needs and threats from rivals. By reinventing A&P four times over some 40 years, the Hartford brothers kept the company way ahead of its rivals by offering customers ever higher levels of value. Once they appointed Burger as their successor, that innovation ended, and A&P declined until it was acquired by a series of owners who kept cutting costs, losing knowledgeable employees, and allowing more successful rivals to win away its customers.

Grocery Industry Case Study Takeaways

The takeaways from these case studies have varying implications depending on where you sit.

Incumbent Executives

- **Do:** Based on the Walmart case, grocery executives may create competitive advantage by
    - Gaining deep insights into the grocery order and retrieval needs of individual consumers in each region where they operate
    - Modifying existing supply chain and retail store networks to match merchandise supply with consumer demand – specifically at each retail store to streamline same-day ordering and pickup
    - Adapting systems to provide timely and accurate information to supply chain and merchandising managers and to consumers regarding order retrieval status
- **Do not:** Based on all the cases, grocery executives should avoid self-destructive tactics such as
    - Focusing exclusively on maximizing cash flow to pay dividends or repay excessive borrowing to finance acquisitions
    - Allowing internal resistance by executives and managers to block the implementation of new grocery concepts that enable the company to offer consumers an industry-leading value proposition

    - Initiating a doom loop of cost cutting to meet quarterly cash flow targets that diminishes the consumer's experience with the store – resulting in lost revenue, poorer product and service quality, and weaker employees

Incumbent Employees

- **Do:** Incumbent employees should seek out the specific jobs that will enable them to contribute to the growth strategies of their current employers or at innovative grocers such as Walmart, Amazon, or Trader Joe's.
- **Do not:** Based on the A&P case, incumbent employees should seek employment elsewhere if they work at grocers that are not creating the future or following fast.

Startup CEOs

- **Do:** Startup CEOs should consider partnering with Amazon, Walmart, or Trader Joe's by developing innovative products they can distribute or technologies that enable them to boost the effectiveness of their online or mobile ordering and supply chain management systems.
- **Do not:** Seek out partnerships with grocery chains that fail to adapt to changing customer needs and the strategies of the most innovative industry participants.

Business Students

- **Do:**
    - Business students interested in developing products that appeal to millennials and affluent baby boomers may consider starting companies that offer innovative products that could be distributed at Whole Foods or Trader Joe's.
    - Based on all the cases, business students should seek managerial opportunities at innovative grocery chains – such as Amazon, Walmart, or Trader Joe's.
- **Do not** work in the grocery industry unless they are passionate about solving its biggest business challenges.

Do You Have the Strategic Mindset of a Grocery Industry Winner?

If you answer in the affirmative to these questions, you have a winning strategic mindset. If not, you must decide whether to change your mindset, strategy, and execution or find a job that better suits your strengths and interests:

- Do you have a deep understanding of the items that its local consumers want to purchase?
- Do you purchase efficiently and operate a supply chain that delivers the items to consumers' homes and enables them to pick up at stores?
- Do you invent new store and merchandising approaches to satisfy evolving consumer needs more effectively than your rivals do?
- Do you have the management skills and technical talent needed to blend seamlessly your physical and virtual capabilities?
- Do you regularly delight consumers so they recommend your stores enthusiastically to others?

Conclusion

The grocery industry is large, growing slowly, and thinly profitable. Yet its importance to human survival – the need for people to eat and purchase food and other items for their families – makes it a compelling industry for companies seeking the opportunity to maximize the lifetime value of many consumers by tapping into their frequent and predictable purchasing patterns. *Create the Future* companies such as Amazon have innovated in the technologies for enabling consumers to order and take delivery at their homes. With its acquisition of Whole Foods, Amazon has opened a new line of products to ship via its Amazon Prime one-day delivery service. Amazon has also inspired Walmart – which executed a *Follow the Leader* strategy of ordering online or via mobile device with pickup at the store or delivery to the home. A&P achieved US industry dominance with its *Create the Future* strategy from the early 1900s to the 1950s – but under *Head in the Sand* leaders, it lost its independence and in 2015 shut down for good. The most important implication for leaders – particularly those in the grocery industry – is that if you lack a *Create the Future* or *Follow the Leader* mindset, hire a replacement who does. Chapter 6 will examine how these three mindsets play out for the furniture industry.

CHAPTER

6

Furniture

The furniture industry was large and profitable populated by many family-owned retailers which faced succession challenges as each generation of the family retired. In general, older family members were poorly suited to reinventing their companies to adapt to changing customer needs, upstart rivals, and new technologies. Moreover, often younger family members in the company lacked the interest or aptitude to lead the company into the future. If a nonfamily member had been groomed to take over, the succession might go smoothly – depending on whether the family members were comfortable with the succession plan. In the absence of such next-generation leadership, furniture industry CEOs faced three options: sell the company to another retailer, sell to a private equity firm, or recruit an outside CEO with the talent needed to reinvent the company.

Whomever next manages the firm, traditional furniture retailers would need to tackle three challenges:

- **A decline in furniture demand resulting from job losses spurring a drop in real estate demand:** By May 2020, 30 million workers had lost their jobs due to social distancing measures aimed at limiting the spread of Covid-19. Few of these newly unemployed would be able to purchase a house – thus capping demand for furniture. While the quarantine created a surge in demand for new furniture from employed people working at home, that demand was unlikely to remain strong in future years. Hence, furniture executives needed to cut back on supply and floor space to meet lowered demand.

P. S. Cohan, *Goliath Strikes Back*, https://doi.org/10.1007/978-1-4842-6519-2_6

- **The threat of market share loss to rivals offering more compelling value to customers:** Online furniture vendors such as Amazon and Wayfair were able to display a much wider selection of furniture through their apps and websites and price and deliver those items more cheaply and quickly than traditional furniture retailers. Traditional furniture retailers could offset some of this advantage by offering an online ordering and store pickup option.
- **The challenge of blocking consumers from showrooming:** Showrooming – a practice we saw in Chapter 2 – was prominent in the furniture retailing industry as well. A consumer could try out different mattresses, for example, at a retailer's showroom and pick the best option. Sadly, for that retailer, the consumer could go online and find another vendor who would sell and deliver that mattress at a much lower all-in cost to the consumer. While matching the lowest online price could be an effective countermeasure, such a strategy could sap profitability.

Furniture retailing is highly fragmented, slowly growing, and reasonably profitable. Like the grocery industry, a few entrepreneurs have developed and executed new business strategies that have resulted in considerable market share gains. As with the grocery industry, entrepreneurs with a *Create the Future* mindset face the considerable challenge of picking a successor with the same entrepreneurial energy. Unlike the grocery industry, furniture retailing is more sensitive to economic fluctuations – if consumers lose their jobs, they defer furniture to finance groceries and are highly unlikely to purchase a house which would need furnishing. The deep economic downturn resulting from Covid-19 social distancing was likely to result in a considerable drop in demand – although virtual retailers could gain market share if retail stores remained closed.

Prior to Covid-19, the store-based furniture industry was doing well with bright prospects. 2019 industry revenue was $64.6 billion with 2.2% average annual growth in the preceding five years. During this period, declining unemployment, increased household disposable income, rising consumer confidence, increased access to credit, and a rising home ownership rate all contributed to increasing furniture demand. Nevertheless, furniture industry earnings before interest and taxes fell slightly – due to increasing wages and price-based competition – from 4.6% of revenue in 2014 to 4.4% in 2019. Due to low mobility barriers, mass merchandisers and warehouse clubs, such as Walmart and Costco, negotiated lower prices by leveraging their higher purchasing volumes – passing those savings on to consumers. Online retailers generated lower sales than traditional ones – $12 billion in 2018 revenues in 2017 online furniture sales represented 14% of furniture sold – but was growing much faster at an average rate of 9.4% between 2013 and 2018, while enjoying rising profitability of 5% of revenue in 2018 (up from 4.1% in 2013).[1] Online furniture retailers – such as Wayfair and Overstock – enabled users to browse a wider selection of furniture which they displayed online without incurring the costs of operating retail stores. Demand for furniture – 95% of which was purchased by consumers – varied by age range, with the lowest demand at the lower price points from consumers under age 25 who tended to rent prefurnished apartments. The most attractive segment was consumers between ages 35 and 44 who were purchasing homes and had enough disposable income to furnish them.[2]

By 2019, the economic outlook for the furniture industry was dimming – even before the economic effect of Covid-19 was beginning to be felt in the United States. IBISWorld expected revenue for furniture stores to increase at a more modest 1.1% annual rate to $68.3 billion by 2024. Although the research firm envisioned rising per capita disposable incomes at a 1.9% annual rate during the period, countervailing forces – such as falling consumer confidence and increased competition – were expected to constrain revenue growth and compress profit margins. With the consumer confidence index forecast to drop an annualized 0.3% by 2024, IBISWorld anticipated that homeowners would become less likely to make large-scale furniture purchases, such as sofas. Due to high levels of competition, price increases were not anticipated – thus capping industry profitability.[3] By April 2020, with 30 million workers having lost their jobs and unemployment reaching Great Depression levels, the furniture industry slowdown appeared likely to accelerate – pushing many store-based furniture retailers into bankruptcy. This industry shakeout was expected to benefit industry leaders who could prevail in online furniture retailing to boost their market share. However, such growth would only flow to participants who had mastered the key success factors – such as competitive pricing, product quality and selection, shopping convenience, website organization and load speed, order processing and fulfillment, order delivery time, customer service, and brand recognition.[4]

Strategic Mindsets of Furniture Industry Winners and Losers

The furniture industry is large and profitable – yet not all participants are likely to survive. In the long term, furniture retailers that fail to find a strong CEO to succeed an entrepreneurial founder may be acquired – possibly with capital from private equity firms – they could file for bankruptcy, or in some cases, they could continue to operate without distinction. The furniture retailing winners will be led by strong CEOs – either founders or successors whose founders planned carefully for the next generation of leadership. Such CEOs will excel at gaining insights into how the needs of their future customers will differ from their current ones. These CEOs will also be skilled at changing their product mix, reinventing their store-based and virtual ordering and fulfillment processes, and improving their approach to hiring, training, and motivating their people so they can increase their market share.

Furniture Industry Startup and Incumbent Success and Failure Case Studies

In the following case studies explored, we will examine how these winning furniture industry practices manifest themselves through three strategic mindsets:

- **Executives with a *Create the Future* mindset were winners:** Executives who were determined to create the future of the furniture industry – specifically, IKEA's CEO Ingvar Kamprad – implemented a strategy based on understanding the specific needs of different groups of customers and adapting its basic operating model, directing consumers' shopping process in its stores to purchase low-priced, ready-to-assemble furniture that they delivered and assembled themselves, to meet those needs more effectively than competitors did. Thanks to its strong culture and effective CEO succession, IKEA continued to follow these principles following Kamprad's departure.
- **Companies with a *Follow the Leader* mindset had the potential to strengthen their market position by tightening operations to become sustainable:** As we will see in the following, the founders of Wayfair were able to build a leading online furniture retailer by acquiring a collection of online furniture purveyors, creating a unifying furniture brand, tracking and analyzing data about consumer behavior, and expanding its product line based on the results of that analysis. Despite Wayfair's success, it continued to suffer due to its inability to generate positive cash flow. Its costs for furniture purchasing, delivery, marketing, and servicing customers were too high as it faced competitive pressure from Amazon. Wayfair's ability to sustain its growth while boosting its operational effectiveness would determine its long-term survival.

- ***Head in the Sand*** **leaders ultimately presided over the bankruptcy of their companies:** Many furniture retailers are family-owned businesses. When the entrepreneurial founder can no longer run the company, their survival depends on whether an entrepreneurial successor is ready to become the next CEO. Below we examine the story of Art Van Elslander who founded a successful chain of furniture retailers, was unable to find a successor who could sustain its success in the face of competitive threats and changing customer needs, and ultimately sold the company to a private equity firm that bled the company dry. Its bankruptcy was a warning to store-based retailers that selling out to financial buyers may help enrich heirs but is likely to endanger their company's long-term survival.

Success: IKEA Creates a World-Spanning Furniture Shopping Revolution

Introduction

In 1947, Ingvar Kamprad, son of a farmer in a poor rural area of Sweden, started a furniture company called IKEA – an abbreviation for Ingvar Kamprad from Elmtaryd, Agunnaryd, his boyhood home.[5] By the time of his death in January 2018, Kamprad was one of the world's wealthiest people – with a peak net worth of $58.7 billion. By 2019, IKEA was generating about $6.4 billion in revenue, with 430 stories in 30 countries and 9.9% market share – making it a dominant player in the furniture retailing industry.[6] Kamprad created the future of furniture retailing with a mindset shaped by a mixture of rural poverty, dyslexia, alcoholism, a hidden fascist past, and a life of near-monastic frugality. Growing up in a poor family on a farm in Southern Sweden, he struggled to concentrate in school and earned money selling matches and pencils in local villages. At 17, he registered IKEA – a mail-order business selling household goods. His thrift and diligence were a mix of truth and fiction – intended to inspire the same in IKEA's employees. To avoid Sweden's high taxes, he lived in Switzerland, drove an old Volvo (as well as a Porsche), only flew economy class, stayed in low-priced hotels, ate inexpensive meals, said his home was modest (though it was a villa overlooking Lake Geneva and he owned a Swedish estate and Provence vineyards), and insisted he had no fortune because the company was held in a charitable trust. He also wrote down his principles for employee conduct in a 1976 book, *The Testament of a Furniture Dealer*, which praised simplicity as a virtue and waste as a sin. Employees were expected to be humble, clean-cut, and courteous, know the company's products, and be enthusiastic about its ideology. Kamprad's name was reported to be in the archives of Per Engdahl, a Swedish fascist, soon after his 1994 death. Kamprad had joined Engdahl's fascist movement in 1942, attended meetings, raised funds, and recruited members. In 1950, he wrote Engdahl a letter which expressed his pride in helping the movement. Once revealed to the public, Kamprad told IKEA employees that he "bitterly regretted" this "most stupid mistake of my life" – blaming his German grandmother's influence. He lived away from other people but traveled around the world to IKEA stores where he anonymously questioned employees as if he were a customer, and customers as if he were a helpful employee. He made no effort to hide his alcoholism – which he claimed to control by quitting booze three times a year. The oft-repeated lore behind IKEA's success sprang from frugality: locating stores on less costly land outside cities, purchasing materials at a discount, minimizing sales staff and enabling customers to shop without pressure, and packaging items in flat boxes with instructions that customers could use to assemble at home. In a 2000 *Forbes* interview, he said, "I see my task as serving most people. The question is, how do you find out what they want, how best to serve them? My answer is to stay close to ordinary people, because at heart I am one of them."[7]

Case Scenario

IKEA's growth was mostly due to geographic expansion and broadening of its product line – however, by 2018 the company had adapted to ecommerce by enabling customers to order online and take delivery at pickup points. In the five years ending August 2019, IKEA's revenues grew at a 6.4% average annual rate to $6.4 billion while its operating income declined a 15.2% annual rate to $352 million. The company was founded in 1943, entered the US market in 1985, and by 2019 operated more than 430 stores in about 30 countries.[8] IKEA blundered when it first entered the US market by assuming that Americans needed the same furniture as its European customers did. They rejected beds and bedding made to metric measure, shallow sofas, short curtains, and kitchen cabinets which were not designed to fit US appliances, tableware, plates, and glasses. IKEA did not stock tables or plates large enough for a Thanksgiving dinner, its particle board was perceived as low quality, and its picture-only assembly instructions frustrated people trying to assemble IKEA's furniture. IKEA eventually addressed many of these issues. Although its $10 table for a college dorm room would not last for decades, IKEA's price/value ratio was competitive. In addition, IKEA began to deliver and assemble furniture, for a price; and it offered planning and design services for customers seeking to outfit a kitchen or home office. Kamprad's principle of staying close to its customers was ultimately not lost on the managers of its US operations. Fearing that it did not understand California's largest demographic group, Hispanics, IKEA designers visited the homes of its Hispanic staff members and added more large-scale furniture, bold colors, and elaborate picture frames to adapt to the needs they observed during the visits.[9]

These principles of adapting to the unique needs of each market helped spur the company's geographic expansion. IKEA opened its first store in India in fiscal 2018 (year-end August) and ended the year with 20 pickup and order points in 11 countries, 31 store distribution centers in 18 countries, and 37 customer distribution centers in 16 countries. By 2019, it employed about 211,000 workers – with 18% of revenue coming from North America (mostly the United States) where it operated more 50 locations. IKEA sold over 9,500 varieties of ready-to-assemble furniture – such as beds, chairs and desks, appliances, small motor vehicles, and home accessories. IKEA used flat packing, which enabled it to reduce transportation costs and sell at competitively low prices. IKEA generated 5% of revenues from food service at its company's in-store cafeterias where it served up Swedish meatballs and free Wi-Fi. By 2018, IKEA had boosted online customer engagement with 2.5 billion customer visits online, more than twice its 957 million physical store visits. While most sales were still done in store, its electronic presence boosted revenue growth.[10]

By 2019, IKEA was continuing to innovate under the leadership of a 20-year executive who became CEO in 2017, Jesper Brodin. Its CFO, Juvencio Maeztu, then emphasized that the company was using the period from 2018 to 2022 to reinvent itself for the next 75 years. To that end, IKEA was trying to adapt to the evolving preferences of young, eco-conscious consumers and rapidly growing digital rivals such as Amazon, Wayfair, and Overstock which were ramping up expectations for service, quality, variety, and price. To that end, IKEA invested in three areas aimed at shortening the distance between the company and its customers: upgrading its digital presence to enable consumers to shop at home in the evening, improving services such as home delivery, and bringing showrooms to city centers. Maeztu explained that IKEA's lower profit was an investment in digital transformation that it intended to continue through 2022. IKEA also aimed to improve its sustainability by reducing the company's greenhouse gas emissions by 2030 and by launching a furniture rental program.[11]

The Covid-19 pandemic accelerated the rollout of IKEA's digital strategy. With consumers quarantined at home, IKEA moved faster to help people redesign and furnish their homes. The pandemic-boosted sales of desks, home organization tools, and children's products. As the pandemic was gaining steam, Brodin was creating IKEA's future with investments in affordable housing, robotic furniture, and a futuristic food cookbook. Moreover, he emphasized that IKEA had achieved 10% market share by dictating what customers should buy and he saw an opportunity to increase that market share by listening and adapting to the specific needs of different groups of customers. To that end, IKEA was building digital channels to reach customers, providing home delivery and assembly, and engaging more directly to learn the specific needs of people in city centers.[12] In March 2020, IKEA added to those consumer-focused digital services by acquiring 3D and visual AI provider Geomagical Labs to enable consumers to design their own homes. The resulting service – which was anticipated to be available by the end of 2020 – would require consumers to photograph a room and upload it to IKEA's platform which would render the photo in 3D. From there, consumers would be able to swap new items in for the old ones and buy what they liked all within the app. Ultimately, IKEA envisioned that the app would digitally place new items into a realistic looking 3D representation of their home, experiment with different styles, estimate a budget, and take suggestions from an AI advisor before purchasing.[13]

Case Analysis

More than any other company in the industry, IKEA created the future of furniture retailing. Kamprad started life with some considerable disadvantages – including growing up in a poor family and suffering from dyslexia and, later, alcoholism and hidden support of fascism. Rather than wallow in his misery, he fought his way out – opening numerous businesses. After he started IKEA, he continued to reinvent its business – adapting effectively to the challenges of introducing his idea into new geographies with differing tastes and buying behaviors. Rather than assume that all customers would view the company as he did, Kamprad emphasized the importance of observing how different groups of customers live and adapting IKEA to their needs. If this mindset continues at IKEA, it may be able to sustain its lead in the industry.

Success: Wayfair Creates an Online Shopping Powerhouse and Struggles to Cash In

Introduction

In 2002, a pair of high school friends who both attended Cornell started an online store that sold bird feeders and other home furnishings. By 2019, that collection of online furniture stores, renamed Wayfair, grew from $450,000 in revenue to $9.1 billion – at a 79% compound annual rate – controlling about 20% of the online furniture market.[14] The company's most notable financial flaw – Wayfair never generated positive cash flow from operations – was burning through $600 million worth of free cash flow in 2019 alone. By April 2020, Wayfair's stock market capitalization was $11.6 billion – impressive, but 28% below its March 2019 high. Driving Wayfair's success were its CEO, Niraj Shah, and his cofounder, Steve Conine. A Pittsfield, Mass. native, Shah's parents both immigrated to the United States from India, which he said, "takes a certain type of entrepreneurial spirit." Moreover, Shah's grandfather was an entrepreneur which inspired him to start a lawn mowing company and paper delivery service. Shah and Conine attended a summer course at Cornell in high school and roomed together as Cornell engineering majors. In their senior year, they took an entrepreneurship class which required them to develop a business plan – for a website development company, Spinners, which did not take off.[15] Shah graduated from Cornell in 1995 and moved to Boston; cofounded an Internet consulting business with Conine, which they sold in 1998; worked as an Entrepreneur in residence at Greylock Ventures; and started and sold a software company. In 2001, he began building a network of hundreds of small ecommerce ventures – such as an online vendor of birdhouses built in the owner's garage which she delivered to the post office.[16]

In the minds of consumers, this collection of companies did not offer a compelling reason to keep buying. In September 2011, they began to solve this problem by taking their first outside capital and changing the name from CSN to Wayfair – which they hoped would become a clear brand that would increase the number of repeat customers. Due to changes in Google's search algorithm, customers were no longer directed to Wayfair's sites out of brand loyalty – for example, purchasers of stereos were unlikely to be frequent repeat buyers. At that point, the company decided to rebrand. While it sent its 700 employees in the streets with Wayfair T-shirts, it was not until 2014 in the wake of airing its first TV commercials – with a catchy jingle – that consumers began to search for Wayfair. By bidding for relevant keywords on Google and savvy use of Facebook, Instagram, and customer emails, Wayfair was able to drive more consumers to visit its site and make purchases.[17]

Shah advised aspiring entrepreneurs to target a huge market, focus on a problem which they passionately want to solve, and help customers quickly when something goes wrong. Wayfair people were bright, ambitious, hardworking, team oriented, and good at analyzing data. Shah believed that if Wayfair hire people who fit with its culture, it could teach them the skills the company needed. Wayfair's culture valued fun and delighting customers. Employees were energized by learning, enjoying their work, and meeting new people. Each team developed its own measurement systems – Shah relied on team leaders to achieve results by trying out creative solutions, getting feedback, and improving. On Friday afternoons, teams shared cocktails, and each month they engaged in group outings to bond with team members such as laser tag and escape rooms.[18] Shah disliked firing people but saw its benefits – saying that the fired employee and the company culture were both better off when it parted ways with Wayfair misfits.[19]

Case Scenario

Wayfair sought growth by providing consumers with a wide selection, competitive prices, rapid delivery, and excellent customer service – however, with 17,000 employees its costs were so high that its operations consistently burned through cash. By 2019, Wayfair envisioned an opportunity to gain market share in the $41 billion online furniture market – as 14% of the $296 billion US home furnishing market had migrated online. Wayfair was targeting a specific group of consumers – the 69 million households earning annual incomes between $50,000 and $250,000. Moreover, as 80 million millennials aged 20 to 37 began moving into houses, Wayfair expected them to purchase home furnishings online. Wayfair offered a wide variety *of merchandise – 18 million products from over 12,000 suppliers. The items varied to suit the taste, style, purchasing goal, and budget when its target shoppers – primarily women in the 35 to 65 age range – were looking to purchase furniture, décor, decorative accents, housewares, and seasonal décor. Wayfair used its "technological and operational expertise" to compete for these customers by providing them with "vast selection, visually inspiring browsing, compelling merchandising, ease of product discovery, price, convenience, reliability, speed of fulfillment and customer service." Wayfair's marketed its products by providing "beautiful imagery and highly-tailored editorial content" and by enabling consumers to decorate their rooms using "Idea Boards" and an augmented reality tool, "View in Room 3D." To fulfill online orders, Wayfair operated with minimal inventory – contracting with suppliers who shipped directly to consumers – while an increasing proportion flowed through Wayfair's CastleGate, Wayfair-owned warehouses closer to consumers from which goods were delivered within two days, and the Wayfair Delivery Network, a method of managing large parcel delivery through consolidation centers, cross docks, and last-mile delivery facilities. To respond to questions from its customers, Wayfair employed 3,600 US-based sales and service people. Wayfair's operations were so costly, however, that it warned investors that it might not be able to generate enough cash flow from operations or borrow enough money to continue operating.*[20]

By February 2020, the flaws in Wayfair's strategy were becoming more apparent. In June 2019, Wayfair employees walked out of its Back Bay Boston headquarters protesting its decision to sell $200,000 worth of bedroom supplies to a government contractor that operates migrant-detention facilities along the US-Mexico border. The enraged employees carried handmade signs that declared, "A prison with a bed is still a prison" and "A cage is not a home."[21] *A securities analyst, Berenberg's Graham Renwick, wrote that Wayfair had fallen behind its rivals on price, selection, and convenience where it previously had prevailed. Renwick argued that Wayfair's best products (out of 14 million items) were frequently available on Amazon at lower prices. He forecast bigger losses for Wayfair as cheaper prices eroded its brand loyalty while it made big capital outlays for fulfillment and to acquire customers. Despite mounting losses, the company had continued hiring, and it received complaints about its high shipping costs for sofas and coffee tables – which included paying for the customer to ship back returns. Critics said that Wayfair's marketing and advertising costs were too high and its customer service needed improvement.*[22] *One Wayfair customer ordered drapes and received a pair that was too long. When he called Wayfair to complain, the customer service rep told him they would send new drapes right away. The agent told the customer to keep the too-long pair of drapes.*[23] *With rising pressure on unprofitable technology companies to make money – or at least detail a clear path to profitability – Wayfair stock was tumbling. Indeed, this was such a well-known problem for Wayfair that two professors published a 2017 paper which found that Wayfair's cost to acquire a typical new customer – $69 – exceeded the $59 that they spent during their entire time as Wayfair customers.*[24] *In February 2020, Wayfair announced it would cut 550* *employees – or 3% of its staff. Shah sent a memo to employees noting, "This last period of investment went on too long. Through two years of aggressive expansion, we have no doubt built some excess, inefficiency, and even waste at times, in almost every area."*[25]

Covid-19 *had a surprisingly beneficial effect on Wayfair. Between its March 2019 high and February 2020, Wayfair's stock had plunged 53% – and it continued to tumble to $22, a whopping 87% below its March 2020 peak. Then, the stock reversed direction. In early April, Wayfair shares soared as much as 51% after announcing that it had enjoyed a sharp increase in sales during the previous month which continued into April. The doubling of its forecast growth rate more than offset investor concerns about Covid-19's interruption of Wayfair's China-based supply chain. Jefferies analyst Jonathan Matuszewski explained that with 80% of store-based furniture retailers closed due to social distancing and Amazon focused on other product categories, Wayfair was enjoying the benefits of consumers spending more on their homes while quarantined.*[26] *A few days later, Wayfair announced mixed financing-related news. It had raised $535 million in a convertible note from two private equity firms. The financing gave Wayfair much-needed cash – but as part of the bargain, the company had to add two board seats for the investors – thus weakening of Shah's and Conine's hold on the company.*[27]

This left Wayfair with good news in the short term and nagging unresolved longer-term questions. In April 2020, Matuszewski saw a significant longer-term growth potential for Wayfair – envisioning a 15% annual growth from 2024 to 2029 while offline furniture retailing shrank at a 1% annual rate. He also described how Wayfair hoped to control its costs to become profitable. Wayfair's growth was driven by customers who were stuck at home with their children buying more stuff. "People are spending more on their homes. They are working on do-it-yourself (DIY) projects. They're buying patio and office furniture, plants, trampolines, swing sets, air hockey games, and storage for small electronic appliances," he said. He also claimed that Wayfair had become more effective at marketing. The combination of three-dimensional imaging of furniture in its in-room mobile app and positive customer reviews resulted in a higher conversion rate. Matuszewski expected Wayfair's operating cash flow to remain "negative in 2020 and 2021." However, he said that Wayfair had set specific cost reduction targets – albeit with slower growth. Wayfair hoped to reduce the ratio of SG&A expense to sales from 13.6% in 2019 to a range from 5% to 7% while reducing its growth rate "from 30% to the high teens, low twenties." This goal would be achieved through more careful hiring; investing with more discipline in projects with high expected returns; and "reduction of the ratio of advertising to sales from 10% in 2019 to a long-term goal of 6% to 8%," he said. By April 2020, questions about Wayfair's future remained: would the initial burst of online furniture purchasing be sustained? Would the abrupt loss of some 30 million jobs by the end of April 2020 drastically reduce home sales – thereby crimping longer-term demand for furniture? Could Wayfair fix its operational problems and lower its costs enough to become cash flow positive?[28]

Case Analysis

Wayfair's success in dominating the online furniture industry was impressive – though its absence of profitability and its lack of product innovation suggest that it was operating with more of a *Follow the Leader* than a *Create the Future* mindset. Two aspects of Wayfair's approach to the industry stood out – its ability to hire and delegate key roles to smart, analytical people and its use of data analysis to make decision about how to set prices and how to decide which merchandise to add, cut, or market more aggressively. Shah was able to persuade investors to share his optimistic view of Wayfair's opportunities and set aside concerns about its inability to generate positive cash flow. Would Wayfair be able to create a new future for online furniture retailing that would extend its lead over IKEA and Amazon? Could Wayfair afford the cost of its liberal return policy – especially when customers did not have an opportunity to try the product in-person before making a purchase?

Failure: After 61 Years, Art Van Furniture Goes Belly Up

Introduction

It is a classic story line: a hungry founder builds a successful business but cannot find the right successor, so he sells out to a private equity firm which runs it into the ground. That is roughly what happened in the 61 years between the 1959 founding of Art Van Furniture, a 169-store, 3,100-employee Warren, Mich.-based furniture retailer, and its March 2020 bankruptcy filing. While there were many causes – including shrinking sales due to loss of market share to upstarts like Wayfair, failed acquisitions, and a burdensome debt load – the fundamental reason for Art Van's failure was its founder's inability to develop or hire an able successor.[29] Art Van Elslander was Art Van's founder. He grew up in Detroit, worked in his father's bar, and sold newspapers as a young boy – taking a job at a men's clothing store when he was 14. After graduating from high school, he joined the US Army, married, started a family, and joined Gruenwald Furniture. In 1959, he opened his own furniture store – dubbed Art Van – a 4,000-square-foot shop in east Detroit. In March 2017, he sold the company – which had since grown to more than 100 stores in five states and about 3,700 employees – to Boston private equity firm, Thomas H. Lee, for some $613 million.[30] At the time of the sale, he said "The time for an ownership transition is right and the opportunity presented itself. There is still much I want to do, and I feel confident knowing the company and its people will be in the best of hands for continued growth and success." At the time of his death at 87, he had a wife, a life partner, 10 children, 32 grandchildren, 4 great-grandchildren, and 1 great-great-grandchild.[31]

Van Elslander understood how vital it was to adapt his company to changing times. At 75, he was struggling to transform Art Van's culture through *Changing the Game*; he was rethinking store design and assessing whether to open smaller mattress-focused stores in small towns. He also admitted to himself that he was an alcoholic and sought treatment – decisions he revealed in a radio interview after checking that his family would not be embarrassed by the public disclosure. In the 1970s, he learned from Peter Drucker that an entrepreneur who kept doing business the way that made him initially successful would ultimately fail. He applied that lesson in October 2005, when he parted ways with Art Van's president for a decade, Bill Barto, who had been with the company for 35 years. Van Elslander and Barto had different views of how to run the company. As Van Elslander said, "One of the most difficult decisions I ever had to make in my entire life was when I parted company with Bill Barto, who was a wonderful, wonderful guy and an excellent, outstanding furniture man. I think it would probably be, oh, easiest said if I said we differed philosophically in what should be done during these very difficult times, and if you aren't marching to the same drummer, you can't run the business." The company's revenues had been declining for years – for instance in 2004, revenues were $545 million – down 1.8% from the year before due to struggles in the automotive industry, a slowing Michigan economy, and increased competition. Van Elslander replaced Barto with his middle-aged sons Gary and Ken. While deciding how to split up the work between them, he said, "I think the boys both have different strengths, they recognize them, and I think they have a great amount of respect for each other. I think they are still going to use Dad as a coach, a little bit." One of Van Elslander's biggest corporate reinventions was his decision to compete with department stores for the bedding and mattress business which by 2005 accounted for over $100 million in revenue – at which time Art Van planned to expand by 40% the size of its mattress department. Van Elslander was also conducting a review of how much store space to dedicate to each product category, opening smaller mattress and bed frame stores in small towns, and leading a *Changing the Game* program aimed at surfacing employee ideas to cut costs and boost sales. An example was providing customers with free in-home design services – intended to boost their furniture and accessory orders. He observed how Drucker's maxim – a failure to innovate and a stagnant corporate culture – spurred the bankruptcies of Montgomery Ward, Kmart, and New York Carpet World. "I see what took place, and what happened, and if you don't change, it's the end of the game," Van Elslander said.[32]

Case Scenario

When he sold Art Van to TH Lee in 2017, Van Elslander thought it would be in good hands – especially since a longtime executive, Kim Yost, remained President and CEO after the sale. Yost had a passion for furniture merchandising and big growth ambitions. He expected the company's new private equity owners to finance their realization. Yost prided himself on being fired early in his career – three times while working for Canadian retailer Woodwards. He was fired once because he decided on his own to rearrange the store's furnishings the way Yost's mother liked it. He hired some friends to move sofas, tables, and lamps on different floors into showroom displays with all three together on the same floor. Fortunately for Yost, an executive – who had seen rivals in High Point, North Carolina, organizing furniture this way – realized that Yost's rearranging was good for business. So, the executive hired him back with a promotion and a raise. An Art Van executive since 2009, by October 2017, Yost was aiming to double revenues to $2 billion by 2021 and to open more stores and create new revenues. Yet he also needed to adapt the company to the changing shopping habits of millennials who spent less on home furnishings than previous generations – $1,500 far below $2,500 spent by Generation X and $3,000 by baby boomers – while buying online. Yost also wanted to introduce a program that would give buyers a discount on new furniture when they traded in the old – a business model started by the auto industry. Yost also tried to encourage innovation by asking employees whether anyone had tried to fire them: if not, he said, those employees might not be pushing enough innovation and change. Yost's ambitious expansion plans included adding new furniture brands, such as Magnolia Home Collections; building 200 new stores by 2021; changing the name of clearance stores to "outlet stores" to attract budget-conscious consumers; boosting from 10% to more than 30% the number of franchise stores; acquiring furniture and mattress retailers; and reinventing its ecommerce operations to achieve $1 billion in online revenue.[33]

Six months after announcing his ambitious plan to double Art Van's revenues in four years, Yost "retired" – only to be replaced by a furniture industry outsider with a track record of short-tenured executive positions. Yost was able to make his mark on Art Van with the November 2017 acquisition of two multigeneration furniture retailers – Pittsburgh-based Levin Furniture, which operated 35 stores across Pennsylvania and Ohio, and Altoona, Pa.-based 115-year-old Wolf Furniture's 18 locations in Pennsylvania, Maryland, and Virginia. With the two acquisitions, Art Van drew a mere $700 million away from Yost's goal of $2 billion in revenues. Yost was proud of the deals, noting, "Today's acquisitions of these two well-established furniture retailers – both intricately woven into the fabric of their communities – underscores a transformative new era of thoughtful expansion at Art Van Furniture. From their commitment to their customers to their long-standing histories and corporate cultures, Levin and Wolf are a perfect fit for Art Van's growing family of brands."[34] *Sadly for Yost, he lost his CEO role at Art Van five months later. Yost's departure followed quarterly declines in same store sales since June 2016 – beginning* *with Art Van's 2013 expansion into Chicago which saturated the market and cannibalized its sales. Following the TH Lee acquisition, eight of Art Van's top nine executives, including Yost, left.[35] TH Lee abruptly replaced Yost with Ronald Boire, who had previously served as CEO at the troubled book seller, Barnes & Noble for 11 months – ending in August 2016.[36] Yahoo! Finance ranked Boire as the worst executive of 2016 after Barnes & Noble reported a $24.6 million loss that year.[37] Jeff Swenson, managing director of Thomas H. Lee Partners, said he was "thrilled with Boire's decision to join Art Van. His deep expertise in retail management and extensive experience leading transformational and omnichannel strategies focused on delivering best-in-class customer experiences – both online and in stores – will be incredibly valuable."[38] By August 2019, Boire was tossed out of Art Van, and a search was begun for a new CEO.[39]*

As a privately held company, it was difficult to know what financial trends were underlying the rapid executive turnover. However, by March 2020, Art Van was bankrupt and soon began completely liquidating its assets. Art Van's core problem was a combination of shrinking revenues and its inability to pay the considerable debts and financial restrictions that accompanied its sale to TH Lee. Art Van's Chapter 11 filing revealed that the company had been acquired for about $613 million – considerably more than the $550 million estimate published in previous reports – and had borrowed nearly $209 million to finance the deal. The filing also revealed that the sale was contingent on a series of sale-leaseback transactions in which stores owned by Art Van were sold to TH Lee – requiring Art Van to pay rent to its private equity overlords. Art Van's Chief Financial Officer David Ladd said revenues declined a cumulative 27% on a same-store basis between 2016 and January 2020. Ladd cited a litany of reasons for the same store sales decline that led to Art Van's bankruptcy. These included competition from online rivals such as Amazon and Wayfair and low-cost traditional furniture retailers such as Bob's Discount Furniture; a revenue-sapping reorganization of showroom floors from product category to lifestyle; $8 million in new furniture tariffs; overexpansion in Chicago; high executive turnover; intense competition in the mattress industry; problems with a St. Louis–based franchisee; and disappointing results from the Levin and Wolf acquisitions.[40] By the end of April 2020, Art Van stores were shuttered due to the Covid-19 lockdown, and on April 7, the company switched from liquidating under Chapter 11 to Chapter 7. Customers who had deposited a total of $35.2 million for furniture they had ordered faced a nasty outcome – they would lose their deposits without receiving the furniture. Nurse Rebecca Breckner had written a check for $21,000 as a deposit on replacement furniture after her Cleveland area house burned down. After ordering new furniture from another store and paying out of pocket, she said, "It's a nightmare. You are telling me that $21,000 worth of stuff is just gone? You do not get anything? It's not normal."[41]

Case Analysis

Art Van Furniture was an impressive entrepreneurial success story with an unhappy ending. Van Elslander was surrounded by sycophants who praised his every utterance. Yet he gave lip service to the idea of reinventing the company to survive without taking the actions needed to stop the company from losing market share. To be fair to Van Elslander, he may have felt insulated from the changes in the industry – such as IKEA's innovative merchandising strategies and Wayfair's 100% online approach to selling furniture. But as we saw in the IKEA and Wayfair case studies, both of them tried out new products and new ways of operating by launching a new idea quickly, gathering data on the level of success or failure of the experiment, investigating the reasons for the success or failure, and trying a new experiment reflecting the learning from the previous one. Art Van Furniture did not use this approach.

What is more, Van Elslander resisted letting go of control of the company – extending his tenure by playing his sons against each other in a family succession battle before hiring in an outsider, Yost, as CEO. If Yost were such a gifted CEO, Van Elslander would not have sold the company to TH Lee which gutted its senior executive ranks – including replacing Yost with a fatally incompetent outsider. Art Van's failure was due to Van Elslander's inability to leave the stage until long after his effectiveness had ended.

Furniture Industry Case Study Takeaways

The takeaways from these case studies have varying implications depending on where you sit.

Incumbent Executives

- **Do:** Based on the IKEA case, furniture retailing executives may create competitive advantage by
  - Creating a strong corporate culture that motivates employees to provide customers with products that meet their evolving needs while providing excellent delivery and post-sales services
  - Building processes that investigate with an unbiased and curious mindset the specific needs of different groups of customers to provide them with good-quality furniture at a low price with timely delivery or pickup and responsive service

    - Introducing new merchandise and purge unpopular products lines while offering consumers new ways to evaluate, order, and take delivery of merchandise
    - Developing executives with the potential to become entrepreneurial CEOs who can sustain its *Create the Future* mindset after the founder departs
- **Do not:** Based on all the cases, furniture executives should avoid self-destructive tactics such as
    - Surrounding themselves with executives who compete to praise everything the founder says rather than challenge the status quo
    - Ignoring operational excellence and financial sustainability to pursue rapid growth
    - Failing to develop a next generation of leadership that can sustain the company's competitive edge

Incumbent Employees

- **Do:** Incumbent employees should seek out the specific jobs that will enable them to contribute to the growth strategies of their current employers or at innovative retailers such as IKEA.
- **Do not:** Based on the Art Van case, incumbent employees should seek employment elsewhere if they work at furniture retailers that are not creating the future or following fast.

Startup CEOs

- **Do:** Startup CEOs should consider partnering with IKEA, Amazon, or Wayfair by developing innovative products these large companies can distribute or technologies that enable them to boost the effectiveness of their online or mobile ordering and supply chain management systems.
- **Do not:** Seek out partnerships with furniture retailers that fail to adapt to changing customer needs and the strategies of the most innovative industry participants.

Business Students

- **Do:**
  - Business students interested in developing products that appeal to millennials and affluent baby boomers may consider starting companies that offer innovative products that could be distributed at IKEA, Amazon, or Wayfair.
  - Based on all the cases, business students should seek managerial opportunities at innovative furniture chains – such as IKEA, Amazon, or Wayfair.
- **Do not** work in the furniture industry unless they are passionate about solving its biggest business challenges.

Do You Have the Strategic Mindset of a Furniture Industry Winner?

If you answer in the affirmative to these questions, you have a winning strategic mindset. If not, you must decide whether to change your mindset, strategy, and execution or find a job that better suits your strengths and interests:

- Do you have a deep understanding of the items that its local consumers want to purchase?
- Do you purchase efficiently and operate a supply chain that delivers the items to consumers' homes and enables them to pick up at stores?
- Do you invent new store and merchandising approaches to satisfy evolving consumer needs more effectively than your rivals do?
- Do you have the management skills and technical talent needed to blend seamlessly your physical and virtual capabilities?
- Do you regularly delight consumers so they recommend your stores enthusiastically to others?

Conclusion

The furniture industry is large, growing slowly, and reasonably profitable. Yet 2020's pandemic economy threw into question many of its basic assumptions – most notably that a strong housing market and a solid economy would generate steady demand for furniture. Instead, the social distancing that was a staple of the world's response to Covid-19 had three major implications for furniture retailers. Store-based retailers were shut down which endangered their survival; over 30 million people lost their jobs which put their families in a cash crisis and slashed furniture demand; and online furniture retailers captured much of the remaining furniture demand for those who were working at home while taking care of their children. *Create the Future* companies such as IKEA and Amazon benefited from these changes. Wayfair – which had a blend of *Follow the Leader* and *Create the Future* mindsets – was also benefiting from these changes, but was threatened by its inability to sustain itself financially. And companies with a *Head in the Sand* mindset like Art Van Furniture found themselves being forced to liquidate all their assets quite abruptly. The most important implication for leaders – particularly those in the furniture industry – is that if you lack a *Create the Future* or *Follow the Leader* mindset, hire a replacement who does. Chapter 7 will examine how these three mindsets play out for the logistics industry.

CHAPTER

7

Logistics

In Chapters 2 through 6, we explored how different CEO strategic mindsets contributed to the success or failure of companies competing in industries that provide products to consumers. For each of these industries, the companies we explored made decisions about which business functions to perform themselves and which functions to outsource to partners. For example, during its early years when it sold books online, Amazon built its own website so customers could place orders online. It relied on partners, such as Ingram, a leading book wholesaler, to fulfill those orders. As the company expanded its product line and dramatically increased its order volume, those fulfillment partners could not meet Amazon's service quality standards – particularly during peak periods of demand. Amazon responded by building its own fulfillment network – consisting of warehouses, trucks, airplanes, and the people and systems needed to operate them. Amazon's decision to backward integrate into logistics has put pressure on its fulfillment partners and changed the structure of the logistics industry. While it began by operating with a few physical assets, the ecommerce industry's ability to fulfill demanding service standards – for example, shipping the right products quickly without breaking them – depends on building an asset-heavy logistics network. Simply put, logistics has become an essential part of ecommerce. That fundamental shift has implications for ecommerce companies, store-based retailers, and the logistics industry. Lessons for leaders include

- **Set customer service quality standards:** It is far more profitable to win new customers and keep them buying than to lure in customers who are disappointed with their initial encounter and decide never to buy again. A customer won't come back if their first order arrives shattered into pieces two weeks later than expected.

P. S. Cohan, *Goliath Strikes Back*, https://doi.org/10.1007/978-1-4842-6519-2_7

On the other hand, if the order arrives intact by the expected time, the customer is likely to buy again – especially if the company already offers the best selection of products at a competitive price. To achieve the benefits of creating and keeping customers over a long period of time, the first step is to set specific, measurable standards for service quality that are higher than competitors'.

- **Assess whether operations can satisfy service standards:** Once a company sets service standards, it must monitor whether its operations are meeting them. For example, a company could set a standard that all orders must be delivered with the products the customer requested, undamaged, within 48 hours. If the company consistently achieves a 100% score for these metrics on its orders, then its operations can satisfy the service standards. If not, the company must investigate the reasons why.
- **Partner or build so your operations can meet your service standards:** If a company is falling short of its service standards, it must conduct a rigorous, methodical analysis of its operations to find the root cause of the service quality problems. Based on that analysis, the company should consider options for fixing those problem causing factors. For example, if the root cause of service delivery problems is found to be with a company's partners, a company should investigate whether it can solve the problem cost-effectively by building its own logistics network.
- **Develop a CEO successor with the right mindset:** The logistics industry has many traditions – most notably, some logistics providers employ unionized workers. Such logistics providers suffer margin compression should they seek to match the prices of rivals with lower labor costs. Given the rising competitive pressure from ecommerce providers such as Amazon, logistics providers must be prepared to rethink and reengineer their strategies and operations to remain competitive with ecommerce providers that backwards integrate. To that end, the boards of logistics providers ought to be developing CEO candidates with *Create the Future* or *Fast Follower* mindsets so that the company is likely to adapt effectively to a rapidly changing future.

These implications emerge from examining logistics – an extremely complex industry based on a simple idea: to deliver goods from their source to their destination quickly and safely. What makes logistics particularly complicated is that this journey can involve many handoffs among different modes of transportation – including ships, airplanes, trains, trucks, and vans – provided by many companies including well-known names such as Maersk, FedEx, and UPS. In this chapter, we will focus on third-party logistics (3PL) – which sorts through all this complexity on behalf of companies. More specifically, 3PLs find the most efficient way to ship goods by providing companies with outsourced warehousing, forwarding, packing, consulting, order fulfillment, brokerage, and transportation documentation. The 3PL industry is a large, steadily expanding, somewhat profitable industry which serves an essential role in most of the industries we have explored in Chapters 2 through 6 of this book. While it is relatively easy to order physical goods electronically, the ability to fulfill orders quickly and reliably is an essential capability for companies seeking to win over new customers and keep them buying. Compared to companies that own and operate asset-intensive services such as trucking, railroad, airfreight, and shipping, 3PL operators are more flexible and less capital intensive – generally with better control over their labor costs.

A more detailed analysis of the 3PL industry reveals that its profit potential is high enough to attract new competitors who can hurdle the industry's relatively low entry barriers. What is more, one of the most vital choices made by 3PL executives is which customers their companies should serve. If they work mostly with fast-growing ecommerce companies, demand for their services is likely to be solid. However, if they depend too heavily on companies that sell through physical stores, revenue growth could be endangered. The 3PL industry grew a 3% average annual rate between 2014 and 2019 to $194.2 billion earning an average net profit margin of 7.4% in 2019. Barriers to entry into the industry were moderate – with a relatively low level of capital intensity (in 2019, a mere 11 cents in capital was invested for every dollar spent on labor). The 3PL market attracted new entrants – with the number of 3PL providers growing at a 3.2% annual rate in the five years ending in 2019. 3PL providers gained a considerable share of increased freight volumes – for example, by 2019 about 53% of total logistics expenditure was directed toward 3PLs – up from 50% in 2017. The reason for the shift is clear: 3PLs were more adept than retail and other in-house transportation operations at keeping up with the growing complexity of the global supply chain and the latest technologies. Moreover, the growing popularity of ecommerce – up at a 13.7% five-year annual rate through 2019 – boosted 3PL demand. Ecommerce's growth increased the volume and frequency of small packages. Moreover, online retailers' desire to expand their logistics and other physical centers made them more likely to outsource to 3PLs. By 2024, forecasters expected the 3PL industry to keep growing – at a 3.6% average annual rate to $232.1 billion – and to generate slightly higher average profit margins of 7.6%. Although new companies were expected to enter the market, mergers and acquisitions were forecast to continue to enable companies to expand globally to satisfy demand from multinational corporate clients, while smaller 3PLs focused on niche markets and offered more in-depth services.[1]

Winners in the logistics industry excelled at four interrelated skills: to control quality, to deploy the latest and most effective technology, to locate operations near customers, and to maintain a good reputation -- which flowed from doing the other three things well. Since 3PLs delivered packages that are valuable and/or time sensitive, the most successful companies operated control systems that kept deliveries from being lost or delayed. Good-quality control depended in part on the ability to deploy technology that boosted productivity and reliability. Broader technological trends were expected to create opportunities for 3PLs that could adopt them to boost efficiency and reliability. For example, technologies that enabled ride sharing could be deployed to match carriers and shippers more effectively. Online ordering systems were essential to matching 3PLs with customers. RFID and two-dimensional bar code technology could boost efficiency by tracking the movement of packages wirelessly. "Snowflake" magnetic ink imprints could allow 3PLs to track and view assets virtually. Finally, 3PLs could use robots to handle, locate, and store packages more efficiently.[2]

In response to the Covid-19 pandemic, in 2020 countries around the world shut down their borders, limited transportation and travel, and thereby put the brakes on the global transportation and logistics industry. These responses hampered important supply chains – with varying effects depending on the mode of transportation, air, freight, and sea – and the country. By June 2020, the gross value added of the global logistics industry had declined 6.1%, while the decline in country logistics markets varied widely – with China reporting a 0.9% decline and Italy suffering an 18.1% decline. North America's sea forwarding market was expected to decline 12.1% in 2020, while the freight forwarding market was forecast to fall 9.5%. Air freight volume was hurt the most – declining 19% in the year ending March 2020. By June 2020, considerable uncertainty prevailed about whether the response to Covid-19 would continue to reduce demand for 3PLs or represent a temporary interruption in this longer-term growth path.[3] One 3PL provider, XPO (profiled later in this chapter), suffered a 6% decline in revenue in the first quarter of 2020 and suspended its forecast for the rest of the year in mid-March 2020 as demand rapidly deteriorated around the time that Covid-19 was deemed a pandemic.[4]

Strategic Mindsets of Logistics Industry Winners and Losers

The 3PL industry was large and profitable – yet not all participants were likely to survive. The economic slowdown in the wake of the Covid-19 pandemic put the most pressure on debt-laden companies with high costs and poorly functioning systems and operations. By contrast, the most successful logistics providers excelled at the key success factors described earlier – deploying technology to build logistics networks that enable them to deliver the right goods reliably, quickly, in good condition to the right location. 3PLs positioned between these two extremes had a short window of opportunity to adapt to the logistics challenges faced by rapidly growing ecommerce providers. 3PLs that could upgrade their services to satisfy their more demanding logistics requirements had a greater chance of surviving. 3PLs that failed to keep up would unwittingly motivate their customers to invest more in their own logistics capabilities – which would endanger the survival of the 3PL laggards.

Logistics Industry Startup and Incumbent Success and Failure Case Studies

In the case studies explored below, we will examine how these winning logistics industry practices manifest themselves through three strategic mindsets:

- **Executives with a *Create the Future* mindset were winners:** Executives who were determined to innovate – specifically, Amazon's CEO Jeff Bezos and its head of logistics Dave Clark – were able to acquire and build technology that enabled Amazon to set and satisfy the highest delivery standards in consumer retailing. Driven by a determination not to repeat its disastrous 2013 holiday season and Clark's obsessive focus on meeting ever higher delivery standards, Amazon was able to keep investing in a complex, multimodal network that made it ever more able to rely on its own logistics networks – leaving its logistics partners increasingly in the dust.
- **Companies with a *Follow the Leader* mindset had the potential to strengthen their market position by tightening operations to become sustainable**: As we will see below, the founder of XPO Logistics – which manages supply chains for more than 50,000 companies in 30 countries – was nimble enough to make large acquisitions that boosted its revenues rapidly. After

making deals, XPO cut costs and improved service quality while allocating capital in ways that generally boosted its shares. XPO also invested in technology to better match shippers and truckers and to optimize pricing. Yet XPO's nimbleness was threatened by the industry slowdown in the wake of the Covid-19 pandemic. Unlike Amazon, which was a clear beneficiary of the social distancing policies enforced worldwide to minimize the spread of Covid-19, XPO's customers were a mix of retailers that were effectively shut down by Covid-19 and ecommerce operators that were beneficiaries of social distancing.

- ***Head in the Sand* leaders ultimately presided over the near bankruptcy of their companies:** YRC – a unionized Kansas City–based provider of less-than-truckload (LTL) shipping services formerly known as Yellow Corp. – was driven into a precarious financial position by William Zollars who took over from the founding family in 1999. By the time he was pushed off the stage in July 2011, YRC had made two large, debt-financed acquisitions, failed to capture the full cost savings potential of these mergers, and allowed its labor costs to remain higher than those of rivals. When the Great Recession dawned in 2008, YRC's revenues plunged some 50%, and the company barely survived. A debt restructuring caused its stock price to plunge over 99%. Despite many efforts to cut costs and restore growth, YRC was never far from another implosion. The industry slowdown that began in 2019 and deepened further in 2020 due to the Covid-19 pandemic made YRC's future even more precarious. By July 2020, YRC had received a below-market rate loan from the government to keep it afloat.

Success: Amazon Builds Its Own World-Class Logistics Capability in 23 Years

Introduction

Amazon was founded in 1994 to sell books over the Web. By 2020, Amazon was a $296 billion company growing at nearly 27% a year with 798,000 employees sporting a stock market capitalization of $1.2 trillion.[5] One of the most significant reasons for Amazon's growth was its logistics network which enabled the company to fulfill its commitments to consumers for timely and accurate delivery of their online orders. As it grew, CEO Jeff Bezos realized that it could only fulfill its commitment to high-quality service if Amazon built and continued to improve its own logistics network. To that end, in 1997 Amazon began operating its own logistics network with two fulfillment centers a 93,000-square-foot one in Seattle and a 202,000-square-foot facility in New Castle, Del. By May 2020, that network had grown substantially – consisting of fulfillment and distribution centers in the United States to process and ship goods including small sortable, large sortable, large nonsortable, specialty apparel and footwear and specialty small parts as well as operating facilities the perform returns processing and 3PL.[6]

Case Scenario

Much of Amazon's logistics expansion was the brainchild of Dave Clark who joined the company in 1999 and became its logistics chief in 2013. Clark was known within Amazon for stealthily identifying and firing workers who were not doing their jobs and for removing obstacles that might keep customers from receiving their orders on time. A case in point was Clark's December 2019 decision to block its third-party suppliers from using FedEx to ship their products due to its slipping performance. Fresh in Clark's mind was Amazon's dismal delivery performance in the 2013 holiday season. Soon after he took over, bad weather and logistical inefficiencies caused Amazon to miss its delivery deadlines, angering customers who demanded and received refunds. To prevent a recurrence, Clark invested billions to build out Amazon's logistics network. By August 2019, Amazon was delivering 46% of US packages purchased on its platform. Although it ended 2019 shipping 2.5 billion packages a year, Amazon lagged FedEx's 3 billion and UPS's 4.7 billion annual packages shipped. Clark's decades of experience give him the ability to sniff out problems in daily reviews of Amazon's operational metrics. He asked the responsible manager to explain the cause of the out of control performance and fix it. Clark also spearheaded the $775 million acquisition of robot-maker Kiva Systems – which saved Amazon's workers from walking miles each day by delivering the products from the warehouse shelves to the workers. By December 2019, Amazon operated some 200,000 robots."[7]

Amazon's logistics network was upgraded to fulfill the promise of its Amazon Prime service which sought to reduce the time to deliver goods from two days to one. Its logistics network included the following components:

- ***Prime Now Hubs**. To provide delivery as quickly as 60 minutes from the time of placing an order, in late 2014, Amazon began to open Prime Now Hubs. These smaller distribution buildings located close to metropolitan centers were stocked with 15,000 fast-selling items.*

- **Grocery logistics.** *Amazon established a different logistics network to fulfill grocery orders – the scale of which was expanded after its 2017 acquisition of Whole Foods. By May 2020, Amazon operated a network of room temperature and cold storage grocery distribution centers across the United States to service Amazon Pantry and Amazon Fresh customer orders.*
- **Inbound Cross Dock (IXD) network.** *To boost the efficiency of the flow of goods into its network of fulfillment centers, Amazon built an IXD network in the United States. The IXD network was located near ports to receive goods from overseas import containers where they were held until an Amazon fulfillment center needed to replenish its inventory – triggering truckload shipments of merchandise from IXDs to fulfillment centers.*
- **Regional sortation centers.** *In 2014, Amazon launched so-called regional sortation centers to gain better control of the outbound shipment of packages within its distribution network. These sortation centers organized outbound packages by zip code before shipping them out of the region via Amazon's Air Hub, to an Amazon Delivery Station, or to the US Postal Service post office responsible for the zip code.*
- **Air gateway sortation centers.** *Amazon also operated a network of air gateway sortation centers near airports that flew customer packages on Amazon Prime Air flights from, say, Seattle to New York. The air hub facilities placed packages from local fulfillment centers into standard air canisters.*
- **Amazon Air Cargo.** *In 2016, Amazon launched its air cargo operation – operating out of 25 regional airports, the company expected to expand its fleet to 70 planes by 2021. Cargo planes flew the canisters from regional airports to a central hub in Hebron, Kentucky, where packages were sorted and sent out to regional airports around the country.*
- **Last-mile delivery stations.** *In 2013, Amazon began building a network of delivery stations aimed at completing the so-called last mile of delivery to consumers. The delivery station sorted packages for outbound routes which were shipped by local couriers who contracted through the Amazon Flex program. Despite problems with Amazon's contract delivery operation, its more than 90% on time package delivery rate was comparable to the performance of UPS and FedEx.*

- ***European Air Cargo***. *By May 2020, Amazon was expected to build out an air hub similar to the one in Kentucky for Europe – likely close to Frankfurt, Germany – which could fulfill an order picked in the United Kingdom to be delivered within one or two days to Spain.*[8]

As Clark focused attention on improving Amazon's on-time delivery performance, the company continued to envision new ways to cut the time and cost of logistics. In addition to dreaming of using drones to deliver packages, Amazon was considering the acquisition of Zoox, a provider of self-driving technology. This possible deal could supplement other Amazon investments in automated driving (Aurora Innovation) and electric trucks (Rivian). A Morgan Stanley analyst forecast that self-driving technology could save Amazon $20 billion a year – about 22% of its estimated 2023 shipping costs. Industry experts envisioned that Amazon could convert Zoox's planned robotaxi into an automated delivery van that could become a mobile version of Amazon lockers. Moreover, Rivian – which by May 2020 had contracted to build 100,000 electric delivery vans for Amazon – could also build the robotaxis. In addition to these acquisitions, Amazon owned 210 transportation-related patents on devices including drones and automated ground vehicles.[9]

Case Analysis

The driving force behind Amazon's logistics network is its CEO's strategic mindset. And the two elements of that mindset were most relevant to how its logistics network was created and how it evolved. Bezos's Day 1 philosophy – that a company must look at its strategy with fresh eyes every day – drove Amazon to build a logistics network that could support ever-shorter times to deliver orders to consumers. Bezos's concept that its customers are delightfully dissatisfied pushed Amazon to make a major investment in its own air and last-mile delivery networks to avoid a repeat of its 2013 holiday delivery disaster. Moreover, because Amazon excels at using technology to serve customers more effectively than competitors, it is likely to continue to expand and improve its logistics network in the future.

Success: XPO Acquires Its Way to 3PL Success

Introduction

Greenwich, Conn.-based XPO Logistics participated in several parts of the $1 trillion US goods transportation industry. For example, it helped provided much of the $700 billion worth of trucking services in 2019 – of that, roughly $600 billion was full truckload and $40 billion was LTL – in which a truck picked up different cargoes and brought them to distribution center, which might ultimately be delivered by another truck to their ultimate destination. Because of the many stops along the way, LTL was more complex than full truckload. XPO used acquisitions to expand *its LTL operations in the United States and Europe. XPO also added multimodal transportation – such as picking up goods at a port and delivering them to railroad terminal.[10] Beginning in 2012, Bradley Jacobs – an industry rollup veteran – began expanding XPO. He did this through a process that was developed by the so-called private equity (PE) industry. Here, debt-backed acquirers dominated industries in which market share was fragmented. PE firms acquired companies with a sliver of equity and big dollop of debt. Such debt-fueled industry consolidation – dubbed industry rollups – was a mixed blessing. It was great for PE investors who used the borrowing to extract dividends and other fees. It also favored investment banks and lawyers who advised the deal makers. But the cash to pay the added debt came out of the hides of employees who lost their jobs in the name of efficiency. Industry rollups could also be bad for customers who looked to these growing companies to invest in innovation that created more value for them. Moreover, PE-backed firms often fared poorly during recessions. As demand for their products plunged, so did their ability to repay the debt. What is more, as we saw in the case of Art Van Furniture, capital providers shied away from bailing them out as their stock prices plunged – often resulting in bankruptcy. This last result was particularly bad for common equity investors – who were generally wiped out in bankruptcy. This comes to mind in considering the growth of XPO. Between 2011 and 2020, Jacobs engaged in a series of acquisitions that led XPO's revenues to soar from $225 million to $16.6 billion, a compound annual growth rate of 61%. By May 2020, XPO was ranked 196th on the Fortune 500 – operating in 30 countries, with 1,506 locations and employing roughly 97,000 employees helping over 50,000 customers to increase the efficiency of their supply chains.[11] Sadly for investors, by June 2020, XPO's shares traded 26% below their September 2018 high, and revenues for its first quarter of 2020 had declined 7% as Jacobs withdrew the company's forecast for the rest of 2020.[12] To be fair, by June 2020, XPO appeared likely to weather the Covid-19 pandemic more effectively than some of its rivals.*

Case Scenario

Jacobs had an unusually large amount of experience with industry rollups by the time he took over as XPO's CEO in September 2011. At 23, Jacobs cofounded Amerex Oil Associates, a New Jersey–based oil brokerage firm, and served as its CEO until the firm was sold in 1983. He entered this business after dropping out of Brown University in the late 1970s. He was fascinated by the profits earned by oil brokers, educated himself on the industry, and cold-called until he was able to persuade an industry legend, Ludwig Jesselson, head of commodity trader Phillip Brothers, to be his mentor. In 1984, he moved to England where he met his oil-trader wife, Lamia, and founded Hamilton Resources, an oil trading company. Using most of his savings and a $1 billion line of credit, he built Hamilton into a $1 billion-a-year company which profited by obtaining oil from Russia and Nigeria and booking ships to deliver the black gold to Europe. By 1989, however, futures markets were squeezing Hamilton's profits, and Jacobs returned to the United States to research *his next company. After reading an analyst's report describing Browning-Ferris's significant profit margins, he interviewed dozens of industry executives to meet talent and identify untapped opportunities. Two former Browning-Ferris managers told Jacobs that the company had ignored rural areas. In 1989, he founded United Waste Systems; Jacobs hired them and ended up acquiring hundreds of small waste management companies in southern Kentucky and Michigan. In 1997, United Waste Services paid $2.5 billion (including debt) for Jacobs's company which had grown to the fifth largest in the United States. As the sale United Waste closed, Jacobs was already working with investment bankers to lead a rollup of the heavy equipment rental business – which he dubbed United Rentals, Inc. (URI). This industry appealed to him because it was fragmented and growing as companies switched from owning to renting equipment such as bulldozers, generators, and scissor lifts. He invested $35 million and in December 1997 took URI public. In 2004, the SEC began investigating URI's accounting practices – two former executives ultimately pleaded guilty to misstating the company's financial condition between 2000 and 2002 to meet earnings forecasts. In 2007, Jacobs – who was not implicated in wrongdoing – resigned as chairman after a failed leverage buyout of the company. By June 2020, URI was valued at about $12 billion.*[13]

Though he had never previously run a transportation company, his previous companies had helped him develop significant transportation and supply chain experience, the ability to integrate acquired companies and grow organically, and the ability to use information technology to connect global offices into a single, smoothly operating network. By 2011, Jacobs concluded that he could use these skills to build a sizeable player in the $50 billion trucking brokerage market. He led a team that invested $150 million in cash in a 3PL named Express-1 Expedited Solutions which he renamed XPO Logistics. His aim was to build a $5 billion to $6 billion annual revenue 3PL provider through a combination of acquisitions and opening of offices in new locations. By 2015, Jacobs aspired to create about 20 so-called cold-start offices with each location generating between $25 million and $200 million in annual revenue a year. XPO also aspired to acquire between five and seven brokerages annually from the 10,000 licensed brokers working with 250,000 trucking companies. In 2012, Jacobs said that XPO's success would also depend on its ability to initiate and enhance relationships with shippers and carriers, and to develop an IT platform extending across its brokerage, freight forwarding, and expedited transport businesses.[14]

Jacobs oversaw XPO's growth in two phases – a series of large acquisitions between 2011 and 2015 and a consolidation and integration phase between 2015 and 2020. In the first phase, XPO spent over $8 billion to acquire 17 trucking, freight brokerage, warehouse management, and online fulfillment companies. Some investors were concerned when XPO paid $3.5 billion in 2015 to acquire Norbert Dentressangle, a French transportation company, and later that year paid another $3 billion to acquire US trucker Con-way. While XPO's stock plunged, it eventually rebounded after XPO integrated the acquisitions, sold Con-way's truckload division, and increased organic growth. In 2018, a short seller *issued a negative report on XPO which again sent its stock down. But by October 2019, XPO was again considering more acquisitions.*[15] *XPO's success was derived from two key strategies. First, the company had achieved a number one or number two market share rank in each of its lines of business. Second, XPO adopted artificial intelligence – which Jacobs saw as a critical new technology – across its businesses. XPO's facilities used predictive analytics and collaborative robots among other tools to provide better customer service by gaining deeper insights into its customers' customers.*[16] *In 2018, 1,700 of its 95,000 employees were working on automating XPO's processes. The projects included pricing algorithms and Uber-like apps that allowed truckers to pick up loads and shippers to track the movement of their cargo in real time.*[17]

In 2020, XPO was scrambling for ways to boost its stock market value. That January it announced plans to remedy what it viewed as its conglomerate discount by spinning off several of its businesses. While XPO planned to retain its LTL operation which handled relatively small freight, units reported to be on the block included its European supply chain, European transportation, North American transportation, and supply chain operations in North America and the Asia-Pacific regions.[18] *That March the stock market collapsed which led to a 54% plunge in XPO's stock price in the month ending March 20 – prompting Jacobs to pull from the market the business units it had planned to spin off.*[19] *By May 2020, Jacobs was focusing on ways to boost XPO's revenues and lower its costs. XPO expected to benefit from strong demand from ecommerce providers. XPO also planned for growth in its truck brokerage business by investing in technology, listening to its customers and employees, and making the technology do what customers wanted it to do. Jacobs also envisioned "ten levers" – such as pricing, applications of technology, and process improvement – with the potential to boost XPO's cash flow by $1 billion. More specifically, XPO's variable costs constituted 77% of its total costs – with fixed costs accounting for the remaining 23%. Jacobs said that he was looking for ways to convert more of that 23% into variable costs. XPO's mission was to create the most shareholder value. Jacobs was willing to do whatever he thought would achieve that aim – including buying back stock; acquiring companies; or using cash to reduce debt.*[20]

Case Analysis

XPO's CEO executed a successful 3PL industry rollup strategy. More effectively than YRC, Jacobs was able to acquire smaller 3PL companies, cut costs, and use common systems to operate the combined companies more effectively while lowering costs. While it ran into challenges – such as declining demand resulting from the world's response to Covid-19 – XPO was able to scramble for solutions more effectively. Whether demand would recover enough for XPO to resume organic growth remained to be seen. Nevertheless, XPO's skills as an effective acquirer of smaller 3PL service providers suggest that XPO was good at conceiving and executing an effective *Fast Follower* strategy.

Failure: Heavily Indebted YRC Struggles to Transcend Its Financial Woes

Introduction

XPO made it look easy to build a big logistics company through acquisition. Not all logistics industry CEOs shared Jacobs's combination of acquisition and operational skills. There are many ways that a strategy of growth through acquisitions can go wrong. Companies can overpay for the companies they acquire; take on too much debt to finance the deals; add new costs that are difficult to cut; struggle to link acquired companies with the parent's systems and processes; and spend so much time on all these internally focused tasks that they fail to recognize and respond to new industry trends and the market share–winning strategies or more nimble rivals. Such problems can turn what sounded like a bold acquisition strategy into an energy-sapping effort to recover from financial blunders that never seem to end – even as new CEOs come in to save the company and quickly depart as their turnaround efforts fail.

This comes to mind in considering the fate of YRC, an Overland Park, Kansas-based trucking company employing 29,000 unionized workers whose stock price peaked in March 2005 at $438,450 a share and by June 10, 2020, had lost more than 99% of its value – trading at some $1.84 a share after reporting sharp declines in daily shipping volume.[21] This massive plunge in value was the result of two reverse stock splits – a 1:25 reverse stock split effective in October 2010[22] and a 1:300 reverse stock split in December 2011 in the wake of a September 2011 $500 million financial restructuring[23] – designed to keep YRC's stock above $1 a share to comply with NASDAQ listing requirements. By the end of 2019, YRC was in financial trouble again. And the Covid-19 pandemic only added to the pressure on the company's shaky financials. The CEO who created this intractable financial puzzle was William Zollars, a 24-year veteran of Eastman Kodak who joined Yellow Corp. in 1996, became its CEO in 1999, nearly presided over its bankruptcy in 2009, and left the company a shadow of its former self in July 2011 before another brush with financial oblivion.

Case Scenario

When he became CEO in 1999, Yellow's revenues totaled $3.2 billion – but growth through acquisitions eventually followed. In 2003, Yellow acquired LTL rival Roadway, which doubled the company's size to over $6 billion in revenue – and it was renamed Yellow Roadway Corp.[24] That move gave the combined company a dominant place in the national LTL market. Analysts thought the $966 million Yellow paid was too high, and they criticized Zollars for failing to take advantage of cost-saving opportunities. Zollars insisted that the companies would operate independently and would keep intact each of their 300 terminal networks. To be fair, Zollars conceded *that some cost would be saved – $45 million in the first year and up to $125 million a year after five years. He also saw the possibility of boosting revenues by persuading Roadway customers to use Yellow's Meridian management services. Nevertheless, Zollars was happy to allow both companies' sales forces to compete against each other.*[25] *Then, in 2005, YRC bought USF Corp., which operated regional LTL fleets. By 2006, YRC – renamed YRC Worldwide – was a $9.92 billion company with $277 million in net income. When Zollars joined the company, it had been run by the Powell family for over 40 years. In 2006, Zollars took a victory lap. In an interview with Institutional Investor, he said that the under the Powell family's leadership Yellow had participated in only one segment of the industry for so long that it had ignored other aspects of the supply chain that affected customers. If a customer told the company it needed a delivery to arrive a day earlier, Yellow told the customer "Sorry, we don't do that." Zollars claimed to have changed the culture by tracking Yellow's reliability, dependability, and service offerings. He said that he spent 80% of his time out of the headquarters visiting workers on docks and dining with customers. It took several repetitions of the idea that Yellow would be consumer driven for employees to be convinced.*[26]

Sadly, for YRC, Zollars's victory lap was premature. As he was bragging of his great management skills, the company imploded – beginning with losses at the end of 2007.[27] *By 2011, its revenues had been chopped in half, and its cumulative net loss exceeded $2.5 billion. At the end of 2009, YRC nearly went bankrupt – being rescued by bondholders who swapped $530 million in debt for about a million newly issued shares.*[28] *Prior to his July 2011 departure from YRC, Zollars tried to frame his tenure in a positive light – noting that his acquisitions created the largest trucking company in the world which brought him praise from the industry. He blamed YRC's problems on the Great Recession which caused revenues to collapse and made it more difficult for the company to repay the high debt load it had taken on to make its acquisitions. Zollars sniped at competitors whose lower fixed costs freed them to cut prices to win market share from YRC. He concluded by declaring that his days in the trucking industry were at an end.*[29]

Zollars's departure did not mark an end to YRC's turmoil. By 2020, after a few more management changes, YRC was still in financial trouble – suffering from a 2019 industrial slowdown and a plunge in industry demand resulting from the world's response to Covid-19. James Welch took over as CEO from Zollars in July 2011. Welch had planned to retire in July 2018 – but was replaced that April 30 by Darren Hawkins.[30] *By December 2019, demand was dropping, and Hawkins's position was looking increasingly vulnerable as YRC appointed a new chair and CFO. YRC reported a 4.5% drop in LTL shipping volume in October 2019 following a swing from a $2.9 million profit to a $16 million loss in the quarter ending September 2019. YRC appointed a banker, Matt Doheny, as chair and replaced its 15-year CFO with Jamie Pierson who Hawkins credited with engineering a turnaround between 2011 and 2016. What's more, three directors quit in what was deemed an "effort to help right-size the board."*[31] *Pierson's tenure featured aggressive cost cutting. Corporate head count plunged* *from 2,200 to under 400 by 2015. In 2013, YRC closed 20 terminals, delayed new equipment purchases, and sold real estate. In 2014, YRC persuaded the union to accept a 15% pay cut and reduced pension contributions for its 26,000 unionized drivers. Soon thereafter, YRC sold $250 million new shares and convertible note holders exchanged them for stock. YRC used the proceeds to pay down debt.*[32]

By May 2020, the world's response to Covid-19 had made things even worse for YRC. Hawkins was scrambling to preserve cash as YRC's credit rating was downgraded. A glimmer of good news was that YRC's first quarter report had improved over the previous year's result -- a $4.3 million profit compared to $49.1 million net loss in the quarter ending March 2019. With lockdowns beginning in March 2020, YRC laid off and furloughed some workers, eliminated executive bonuses and merit raises, and cut capital spending. Lenders agreed to defer some interest payments and suspended a covenant requiring YRC to maintain at least $200 million in adjusted earnings before interest, taxes, depreciation, and amortization. YRC missed a March payment to a multiemployer health-care fund covering some 500,000 Teamster members. On March 31, Moody's Investors Service cut its ratings for YRC – citing its weak credit profile and thin margins.[33]

YRC's position continued to deteriorate. In July 2020, the Treasury lent YRC $700 million in exchange for about 30% of YRC's stock. On July 1, when the loan was announced, YRC's stock had fallen 27% during the year and was valued at $70 million. The loan was justified by saying that YRC – which ships freight for the US military – was critical to national security. At the same time, the Defense Department was suing YRC for overcharging in the millions of dollars over seven years for its services and failing to follow government procurement rules.[34]

Case Analysis

YRC is a story of an acquisition strategy gone so badly that it defied the efforts of many CEOs to fix it. Ultimately YRC's problem was taking on too much debt to acquire rivals in pursuit of a rapid increase in revenues. While the short-term ego rewards to YRC's CEO were high, the company failed to properly integrate the companies it acquired. This resulted in costs that were too high – because the CEO failed to cut overlapping operations – and a failure to integrate the acquired companies into the parent company's systems and processes. Moreover, YRC's unionized workers earned high compensation relative to those of YRC's rivals – which made it easier for rivals to win its customers by cutting price. YRC could not set its prices lower without sacrificing its profit margins. After a financial restructuring that wiped out most of its shareholders' equity, YRC stock has remained exceptionally low for years. Covid-19 has made hopes for its recovery even more difficult to imagine.

Logistics Industry Case Study Takeaways

The takeaways from these case studies have varying implications depending on where you sit.

Incumbent Executives

- **Do:** Based on the Amazon and XPO case, logistics executives may create competitive advantage by
  - Setting ever-shorter delivery time targets and investing in the logistics networks needed to meet those standards reliably
  - Analyzing process inefficiencies that cause delivery problems and seeking out and acquiring or building new technologies that can fix these inefficiencies
  - Building and using systems to track in real time critical operating metrics related to satisfying commitments to customers
  - Hiring and developing managers and staff who can take responsibility for identifying the causes of delivery problems and deploying effective solutions
- **Do not:** Based on all the cases, logistics executives should avoid self-destructive tactics such as
  - Surrounding themselves with executives who seek to retain their jobs by praising the CEO's pronouncements rather than challenging the status quo
  - Ignoring operational excellence and financial sustainability to pursue rapid growth
  - Failing to develop a next generation of leadership that can sustain the company's competitive edge

Incumbent Employees

- **Do:** Incumbent employees should seek out the specific jobs that will enable them to contribute to the growth strategies of their current employers or at innovative logistics providers such as Amazon or XPO.
- **Do not:** Based on the YRC case, incumbent employees should seek employment elsewhere if they work at logistics providers that are not creating the future or following fast.

Startup CEOs

- **Do:** Startup CEOs should consider partnering with Amazon by developing innovative technologies that these large companies can use to make their logistics operations more efficient and effective.
- **Do not:** Seek out partnerships with logistics providers that fail to adapt to changing customer needs and the strategies of the most innovative industry participants.

Business Students

- **Do:**
    - Business students interested in logistics should start companies that can solve the most pressing operational problems facing innovative logistics suppliers such as Amazon or XPO.
    - Based on all the cases, business students should seek managerial opportunities at innovative logistics suppliers such as Amazon or XPO.
- **Do not** work in the logistics industry unless they are passionate about solving its biggest business challenges.

Do You Have the Strategic Mindset of a Logistics Industry Winner?

If you answer in the affirmative to these questions, you have a winning strategic mindset. If not, you must decide whether to change your mindset, strategy, and execution or find a job that better suits your strengths and interests:

- Do you have a deep understanding of the logistics expectations of your business customers?
- Do you operate a logistics network that can satisfy customers' delivery expectations reliably and at a competitive price?
- Do you invent or acquire new technologies that enable you to outperform your competitors at satisfying your customer's delivery time, quality, and price expectations?
- Do you have the management skills and technical talent needed to analyze and solve operational problems in real time?
- Do you regularly delight customers, so they recommend your logistics service enthusiastically to others?

Conclusion

The logistics industry is large, growing slowly, and reasonably profitable. Yet 2020's pandemic economy reduced demand for logistics suppliers other than those who served ecommerce leaders – such as Amazon – which enjoyed a surge in demand as store-based retailers temporarily shut down and reopened with much lower business volumes. *Create the Future* companies such as Amazon benefited from these changes. *Follow the Leader* companies like XPO were in an uncertain position – depending on whether more its demand came from customers were Covid-19 winners, rather than losers. And companies with a *Head in the Sand* mindset like YRC found themselves in a precarious financial state. The most important implication for leaders – particularly those in the logistics industry – is that if you lack a *Create the Future* or *Follow the Leader* mindset, hire a replacement CEO who does. Chapter 8 will examine the implications of CEO strategic mindset for leaders.

PART

II

Implications for Leaders

CHAPTER

8

Leading Through Strategic Mindset

In this book, we have seen the power of a CEO's strategic mindset to change the company's culture, strategy, and operations – which ultimately improved the company's performance and prospects. Here are some examples of how that dynamic operated:

- **From company *Head in the Sand* decline to *Fast Follower* growth:** In 2012, when Hubert Joly took over as Best Buy's CEO, the company was losing ground to Amazon and posted a huge loss. By the time Joly handed over the reins to his successor in 2019, the company was earning a profit, and its stock had soared 330%. Joly's mindset was not to maximize profit but to create meaning for Best Buy's employees so they would be inspired to

P. S. Cohan, *Goliath Strikes Back*, https://doi.org/10.1007/978-1-4842-6519-2_8

think up and deliver its customers the best experience in the industry. This mindset drove Joly to change Best Buy's culture, match etailers' lower prices, partner with rivals such as Amazon, and change employee incentives to encourage them to deliver and industry-leading customer experience.

- **From *Create the Future* industry dominance to *Head in the Sand* irrelevance:** John and George Hartford took over a small grocery store chain from their father and turned A&P into the largest grocery retailer in the United States with 16,000 grocery stores in 3,800 communities. The Hartfords were persistent experimenters – testing out different store concepts to satisfy changing consumer needs and rolling out the most effective innovations – all with greater speed and effectiveness than did competitors. They created the future of grocery retailing, and when they retired, they put their stock into a trust and appointed Ralph Burger, a long-term loyal employee, to run the company in 1951. To finance dividend payments, Burger starved investment in new retail concepts. Burger's *Head in the Sand* mindset made A&P increasingly irrelevant to consumers. In 1979, A&P was sold to a German retailer, and by 2015 it went bankrupt for the second and final time after rounds of cost cutting failed to boost its revenues and cash flow.
- **From *Create the Future* leadership in one market to *Create the Future* leadership in others:** More than any CEO discussed in this book, Amazon founder and CEO, Jeff Bezos, epitomizes the power of a CEO's strategic mindset to create the future of previously disparate industries. Bezos's strategic mindset rests on two ideas: his Day 1 philosophy of fighting complacency by emphasizing the importance of not relying on past approaches to solve future problems and the need to keep inventing ways to delight its easily dissatisfied and demanding consumers. Based on these two ideas and the way they changed Amazon's strategy and operations, the company has gone from an online bookstore to a world leader in consumer ecommerce – carrying an estimated 353 million different products; operating a fast-growing logistics network; and creating and continuing to dominate the cloud services industry. Bezos's mindset has caused Amazon to try countless

experiments, measure outcomes, learn from mistakes, hire and develop talented people, and build world-class capabilities to enable Amazon to dominate the industries in which it competes.

Outside the scope of this book, there are other permutations of how changes in CEO mindset can alter a publicly traded company's performance and prospects. Here are some others from outside the technology industry:

- **From a *Create the Future* founder whose confirmation bias turns him into a *Head in the Sand* failure:** A founder's success can lead to failure. More specifically, the strategic mindset that enables a founder to build a successful, public company can reinforce a strong bias toward what leads to strategic success in the industry. If new technologies alter the basis of success, that founder's strategic mindset can cause the founder to ignore the new technologies – enabling the purveyors of those innovations to take its customers. This is what happened to Digital Equipment founder and CEO Ken Olson when he dismissed the importance of the PC and the Internet. His *Create the Future* mindset evolved into a *Head in the Sand* one. Indeed, this tendency of success to lock in a founder's initial understanding of how to compete in the industry is the reason why Bezos's Day 1 idea is so important and powerful – if a leader can follow it.
- **From a *Create the Future* founder to a *Head in the Sand* successor to a *Fast Follower* replacement who accelerates growth:** This is what happened to Microsoft when Bill Gates handed over the reins to his number two, Steve Ballmer – a *Head in the Sand* CEO who pushed Windows-first. Fortunately, Microsoft survived Ballmer and has done much better under his successor, Satya Nadella, a *Fast Follower* who changed Microsoft's culture to put the customer first and enabled its products to work alongside competing ones had previously built Microsoft's Azure cloud business into a formidable challenger to AWS. As of June 2020, Nadella's nearly seven-year tenure as Microsoft CEO boosted its shares at a 29% average annual rate, leaving the company's stock roughly four times higher than its previous peak when Bill Gates was CEO. Nadella also presided over modest revenue growth – up at an 8.3% annual rate through 2019 to $126 billion. This example makes it clear

> that just because he had been Gates's number two for years, Ballmer was not best leader for Microsoft because he applied his old way of thinking to solve new problems. Nadella has proven to be more effective because he has changed Microsoft enough to apply its strengths to competing with Amazon and other more innovative rivals.[1]

Strategic Mindsets for Public and Pre-IPO Companies

These case studies suggest a simple model that public company directors might consider when thinking about how to choose a new CEO with the right mindset to capture future opportunities and/or defend against threats facing the company. As illustrated in Figure 8-1, the Amazon board may wish to consider three strategic mindsets for a successful *Create the Future* CEO such as Jeff Bezos. While a *Create the Future* successor might envision a radically different strategy for Amazon, such a successor might be so disruptive to Amazon's current culture that there could be high turnover in key leadership team roles – thus making it very difficult or at a minimum sharply delaying the implementation of the successor's new vision. A *Follow the Leader* successor would be more likely to find and capture growth opportunities within the founder's vision – but might struggle to envision and gain significant revenues from a fundamentally new growth opportunity. Finally, as the Hartford Brothers did with Berger, Bezos might insist on appointing a *Head in the Sand* successor who would harvest Amazon's cash-generating businesses and pay dividends to Bezos and other major shareholders. This cash cow–milking approach would result in Amazon's loss of market share and pave the way for rivals to pick up the slack.

Figure 8-1. Amazon CEO Successors: Benefits and Risks of Three Strategic Mindsets

What many of these public companies have in common is that their founders were what I call marathoners[2] – founders who grow their companies from an idea to a large public company. Few of today's marathoners have gone the distance without the help of venture capital firms. Such marathoners include Eric Yuan, CEO of Zoom Video, and Peter Gassner, founder and CEO of pharmaceutical and life sciences cloud software provider Veeva Systems. Both have proven to be adept at growing revenue, taking their companies public, and boosting their stock price. Yuan's leadership benefited Zoom's employees, customers, and shareholders. Between 2017 and 2020, Zoom's revenues grew at a 117% annual rate from about $61 million to $623 million. From its April 2019 IPO and June 2020, Zoom shares soared at a 198% annual rate to $258. Gassner also did an excellent job shifting from founder to public company CEO. Between 2012 and 2020, Veeva's revenues grew at a 43.6% annual rate from about $61 million to $1,104 million. From its October 2013 IPO to June 25, 2020, Veeva shares rose at a 29% annual rate to $236.[3]

To turn an idea into a large publicly traded company, the skills demanded of a CEO vary by the firm's stage of scaling. As depicted in Figure 8-2, a company founder must develop new skills in order to become a so-called forever CEO – one like Jeff Bezos who can turn an idea into an industry-leading publicly traded company that keeps growing at over 20% a year. Private company directors ought to assess whether the current CEO can develop the skills needed to excel at the next stage of scaling. If not, the board must seek a replacement who will fit within the culture and have a track record of having mastered the skills needed to take the company public.

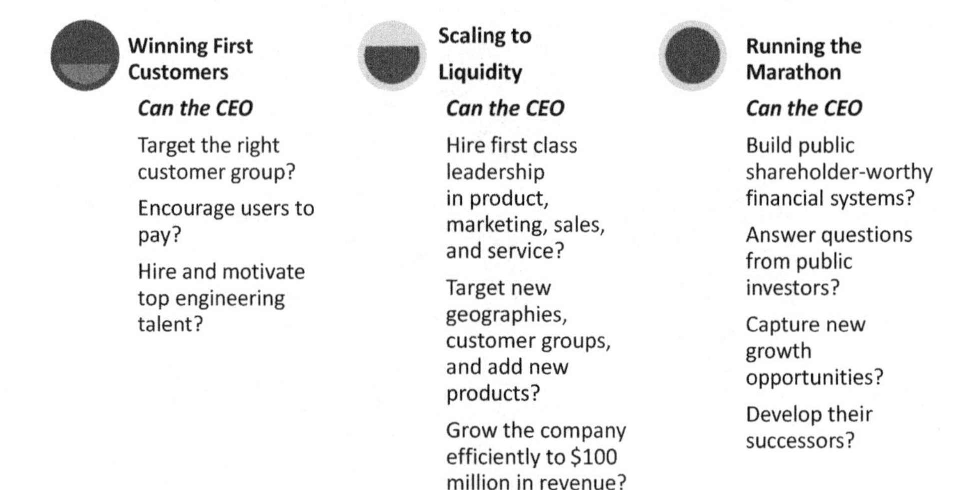

Figure 8-2. CEO Skills Required at Three Stages of Scaling from Idea to Public Company

Interestingly, some successful venture capitalists are good at finding founders with the right personal traits – such as motivation, grit, passion for winning, and the ability to motivate diverse teams – needed to learn these skills as the company grows. Emergence Capital Partners' General Partner, Santi Subotovsky, explained in a June 2020 interview, "When we assess CEOs and leaders in general we work hard to get to the bottom of their motivations as we find a high correlation between this and success. We also have the advantage of having seen leaders like Yuan and Gassner early in their journeys." Emergence looks for CEOs who have unique personalities. "Leaders building iconic companies are typically irrationally obsessed; they have a strong conviction about how the future should work, and they don't stop until their visions become a reality. These CEOs will work intensely to make this happen and as a result they will weather the storms that are part of the company building journeys," noted Subotovsky. Chris Lynch, a startup investor and CEO of data virtualization provider AtScale, sees hunger and competitive drive as among the critical traits for a founder who can grow from an idea to taking a company public. As he told me in June 2020, "Fewer than 50% of company founders are still CEO when the company goes public. I have one company, artificial intelligence platform DataRobot, that has gone from $0 to $100 million in revenue with the original CEO. He is impatient with stupid questions so he would not like talking to a hedge fund analyst who owns the company's stock. He has technical chops and vision. And he has [grit] after overcoming poverty and other challenges. He is self-aware and intensely competitive. He has leadership skills. He knows how to motivate engineering, sales, and marketing. He has the x-factor: blind ambition. He wants to build the next Google and is willing to sacrifice his personal life to get there."[4] Another venture capitalist and board member, Michael Greeley, General Partner of Flare Capital Partners, told me in July 2020, that founders who can turn an idea into a public company share unique traits. They "hear the voice of the customer – e.g., know what the customer is looking for, have the technical skills to build the product, and are pied pipers who can [attract and motivate] talent."[5]

The board of directors should play a crucial role in determining the fit between the CEO and the opportunities and threats that await in a company's future. However, if the directors do not think and act independently, the company's investors, employees, and customers could be at risk. To avoid crimping directors' independence, CEOs must keep their egos in check and recruit a talented board that will protect the interests of these important stakeholders by encouraging fact-based debates regarding what the company should do about its company's opportunities and threats. Board compensation can influence whether this debate really happens. If a company pays board members nearly $600,000 a year to attend four board meetings, as Salesforce does, there is a risk that board members will refrain from asking the CEO challenging questions to preserve their seat on the money train. To counter this problem, Lynch pays directors solely in stock options. As he told me in a June 2020 interview, "This is how I pay directors. It's a lot more work for them than public boards because the only way to make the options worth anything is to grow the company and take it public."[6]

Independent directors should leave the management of the company to the CEO; however, they should do four things:

- **Focus the company on its most important strategic issue:** That could be the risk of missing a growth opportunity or the failure to address a threat to its survival. As Harvard Business School Associate Professor, Laura Huang, said in June 2020, "Directors should start by deciding what problem the company needs to solve: opportunity gap – the company has an opportunity that it is not fully capturing – or problem gap – the company is facing a threat to its survival or market position and lacks an effective solution or has not executed it properly. Directors need to know where the company is now and where the industry is headed."
- **Assess whether the CEO can hurdle each of the three stages of scaling:** If a CEO cannot make it to the next stage, directors will put him in a tight spot. That is what happened to then 36-year-old Lynch six months before ArrowPoint Communications's March 2000 IPO. The company's lead director, venture capitalist Paul Ferri, invited Lynch to breakfast and told him to recruit the more shareholder-friendly CEO Ferri had in mind. Lynch's "ears were burning" but he did as Ferri directed. In May 2000, Cisco acquired ArrowPoint for $5.7 billion – turning Lynch's 1.2% stake in ArrowPoint into some $68

million worth of Cisco stock. Greeley pointed out that such decisions typically are made in conjunction with an effort to raise capital. He said, "Every 15 to 18 months, our portfolio companies need to raise capital. If they meet with 20 investors and receive no interest, it triggers a conversation with the CEO. We ask them bluntly, 'Do you want to be rich or king?' If they choose rich, they are more likely to be willing to step into a founder and chief technology officer role and let a new CEO take over who can raise the capital and keep the company growing."

- **Encourage the CEO to execute a succession plan:** Directors should encourage the CEO to develop successors. After all, at least half of company founders are no longer CEO by the time it goes public. To do that, they should hire people who have succeeded in similar companies and put them in a position where they can take on greater responsibilities. It generally works better to develop internal candidates – something that Walmart does well, according to Stanford Business School Professor Charles A. O'Reilly III. As he told me in June 2020, Succession 101 means boards should ask, "Does the [CEO candidate] have a good grasp on industry dynamics, think long-term, and drive large-scale organizational change?" To be sure, developing a successor internally helps mitigate the risk that an outside CEO will be rejected by the culture. But that cultural fit can also mean the company adapts too slowly. Walmart's slow adoption of ecommerce is a case in point. After all, the giant retailer launched Walmart.com in 2000[7] and 16 years later had still not grown the business enough, so it paid $3.3 billion to acquire Jet.com as a way to hire its CEO Marc Lore[8] – suggesting that sometimes an internally developed CEO is not always able to accelerate an incumbent's growth.

- **Track the right performance metrics:** Directors ought to monitor longer-term and short-term performance metrics. They should ask the CEO questions about trends that are significantly worse than expected – with the focus on what is causing the company to miss its numbers and what the CEO will do to get the company back on track. Those metrics will vary depending on the company's growth stage. For public or large private companies, directors should ask the CEO to explain declining financial performance, new competitors successfully taking away market share, and new technologies that might alter the competitive landscape, said O'Reilly. Board members of a technology company that is sprinting to liquidity should focus on "development productivity, employee recruitment and retention, gross margins, customer acquisition, annual recurring revenue, customer churn and profit," Lynch said.[9]

How a Change in Strategic Mindset Helps Goliath Strike Back

The idea behind the David and Goliath story is that a small, agile fighter can overcome the perceived superior strength of the giant by taking advantage of its slower response time. While this story is an apt parable for the competitive dynamic between an incumbent and an upstart, the point of this book is that depending on the CEO's strategic mindset, a Goliath can adapt to the competitive threat from an upstart – thus building on its strengths to add rapidly to its market share. Conversely, an upstart's success can make it overconfident – causing its CEO to mimic the incumbent's ponderous response to new opportunities and threats – which ultimately leads to the upstart's loss of market share. As illustrated in Figure 8-3, the CEO's strategic mindset determines how well a company responds to external factors that alter its ever-changing array of opportunities and threats. To illustrate how this works in practice, consider how the Covid-19 pandemic affected Wayfair (which we examined in Chapter 6). Simply put, Covid-19 was a sudden boon to Wayfair's business. While its strategic mindset did not change, the pandemic presented a growth opportunity, and thanks to a concomitant disappearance of many active rivals and its very good positioning vis-à-vis customer expectations, Wayfair benefited tremendously. Here's how:

- **Changing opportunities and threats:** Covid-19 abruptly changed the matrix of opportunities and threats facing Wayfair. In the latter few months of 2019 through March 2020, demand for furniture was growing only modestly. WeWork's busted IPO resulting from its cash flow–burning business model and shareholder-unfriendly governance led investors to lose faith in the company's ability to find a path to positive cash flow. Wayfair's stock was plunging. Yet Covid-19 caused a feeding frenzy for furniture as millions began working from home. While stocks plunged in March 2020, investors gobbled up shares of companies that enjoyed accelerated revenue growth due to Covid-19. Between their bottom in March and June 2020, Wayfair shares soared more than eightfold.

- **CEO mindset:** Wayfair CEO Niraj Shah's strategic mindset was that of a *Fast Follower*. To Shah's credit, he built a leading online furniture retailer by acquiring a collection of online furniture purveyors, creating a unifying furniture brand, tracking and analyzing data about consumer behavior, and expanding its product line based on the results of that analysis. Yet Shah had his limitations since Wayfair continued to suffer due to its inability to generate positive cash flow and its excessively high costs – for furniture purchasing, delivery, marketing, and servicing customers.
- **Competitive strategy:** Wayfair's competitive strategy did not suddenly change when Covid-19 happened. However, its competitive environment abruptly became more favorable because store-based furniture retailers were shut down due to social distancing and Amazon's attention was distracted as it ramped up capacity to meet the surge in demand for more basic goods such as masks and hand sanitizers. Wayfair captured a large share of that surge in demand because it was already popular with consumers due to its ability to satisfy customer purchase criteria such as wide product selection, reasonable prices, and generally good service – marred slightly by flawed execution of its return policy.

Figure 8-3. Strategic Mindset and Competitive Strategy

While Wayfair benefited from Shah's *Fast Follower* strategic mindset, its competitive strategy, and its abruptly improving opportunity and threat matrix, directors must anticipate how the CEO's strategic mindset might cause performance-destroying misalignments between outside forces and the company's strategy. The cases summarized in Figure 8-4 suggest that strategic mindset can play an important role in whether a company's competitive strategy adapts effectively to new opportunities and threats. Alignment among the three results in faster revenue growth and stock price – while misalignment drives less favorable outcomes. Comparing the fate of Netflix and Blockbuster helps illustrate this pattern. Blockbuster went bankrupt in 2010 as Netflix was beginning its successful surge. As we saw in Chapter 3, John Antioco, one of many Blockbuster CEOs appointed in the wake of its acquisition by Viacom, was slow to introduce a DVD rental service and turned down a 2000 opportunity to acquire because he did not see digital media as a threat to Blockbuster's retail store–based DVD rental business. Contrast Antioco's *Head in the Sand* mindset to Hastings's realization that video streaming was a threat to Netflix's DVD-by-Mail business. Rather than allow video streaming to swipe Netflix's subscribers, Hastings launched a PC-based online streaming service in 2007 – the year Apple launched the iPhone. As wireless broadband became more widely available and the iPhone and iPad were widely adopted, Netflix invested more heavily in its online streaming business. Faced with the possibility of providing consumers with video entertainment via online streaming, Hasting's *Create the Future* mindset enabled to make that Netflix's core source of revenue, while Antioco's *Head in the Sand* mentality led Blockbuster to dismiss online streaming's significance and remain locked into its debt-laden retail store–based video rental business strategy.

	New Opportunity	New Threat
Create the Future	**Bezos/Amazon:** Cloud, Prime, etc. (Stock +37.6%/year May 1997 to July 2020)	**Hastings/Netflix:** Online streaming (Stock +41%/year January 2007 to July 2020)
Fast Follower	**Nadella/Microsoft:** Cloud (Stock +29%/year February 2014 to July 2020)	**Cook/Apple:** iPhone rivals (11.6% annual revenue growth 2011 to 2020 vs. 21.4% 1997 to 2011)
Head in the Sand	**Antioco/Blockbuster:** DVD-by-Mail, Online Streaming (Bankrupt 2010)	**Olson/DEC**: PC, Internet (Merged with Compaq for $9.6B in January 1998)

Figure 8-4. Assessing Alignment Between Strategic Mindset, New Opportunity/Threat and Performance

A Two-Phased Approach to Leading Through Strategic Mindset

How can a change in strategic mindset help Goliath fight back? In theory, the company's board should help its CEO to formulate, evaluate, and execute strategies that will capture opportunities and defend against threats. In practice, there are many dysfunctions in the relationship between the board and the CEO. These include

- Some board members are reluctant to challenge the CEO wanting to hold onto their lucrative sinecures.
- Some board members are heirs of the founders who feel entitled to dividends and lack knowledge of the company's business.
- Some board members had valuable knowledge and contacts when they joined the board – however, the industry has changed, and they have not kept up.
- Board members who were appointed by the current CEO and feel uncomfortable asking the CEO for a succession plan or discussing the possibility of replacing the CEO.

To help readers assess whether their company is leading effectively through strategic mindset, what follows is an idealized version of how the board and CEO ought to interact. The value of this model is that it can help highlight where a company is falling short and help point out specific improvement opportunities as it seeks to ensure that its CEO's strategic mindset is suited to crafting a competitive strategy that can capture opportunities and protect against threats likely to emerge in the future.

To overcome these challenges, incumbent company boards and CEOs should engage in two broad processes:

- **Develop a competitive strategy to close the problem/opportunity gap:** As illustrated in Figure 8-5, a company's board should heed Huang's advice and identify the primary issue facing the company. This could be either closing the *opportunity* gap, for example, adopting a new technology or new business model that would enable the company to gain market share rapidly, or the *problem* gap, for example, reversing a slide in revenue and cash flow due to a plunge in demand resulting from social distancing. Having identified the primary corporate issue, the board would challenge the CEO – granting resources such as hiring a consulting firm or staffing a strategic planning function – to formulate options, choose a competitive strategy, and defend the strategy before the board.

- **Assess the fit between the competitive strategy and CEO's strategic mindset:** As illustrated in Figure 8-6, the board would use the competitive strategy exercise to assess whether the CEO's strategic mindset is well suited to closing the company's problem or opportunity gap. The board should evaluate the CEO's competitive strategy on two dimensions: the quality of the vision and the company's ability to execute the vision. If the board determines that the vision and execution of the CEO's competitive strategy are excellent, then the company should encourage its current CEO to implement the strategy. If the board deems the vision excellent, but the execution deficient, then the board should consider hiring a new CEO with a *Fast Follower* mindset – or possibly hiring a chief operating officer who can improve on and execute the strategy's implementation plan. If the board gives a poor grade to the strategy's vision but a high score for its execution, then the company should consider hiring or appointing a *Create the Future* CEO and ask the current CEO to partner with the new one as chief operating officer. Finally, if the board finds both the vision and execution of the competitive strategy to be unacceptable – or concludes that the company's culture is dysfunctional – then the company should bring in a new CEO who has either a *Create the Future* or *Fast Follower* mindset.

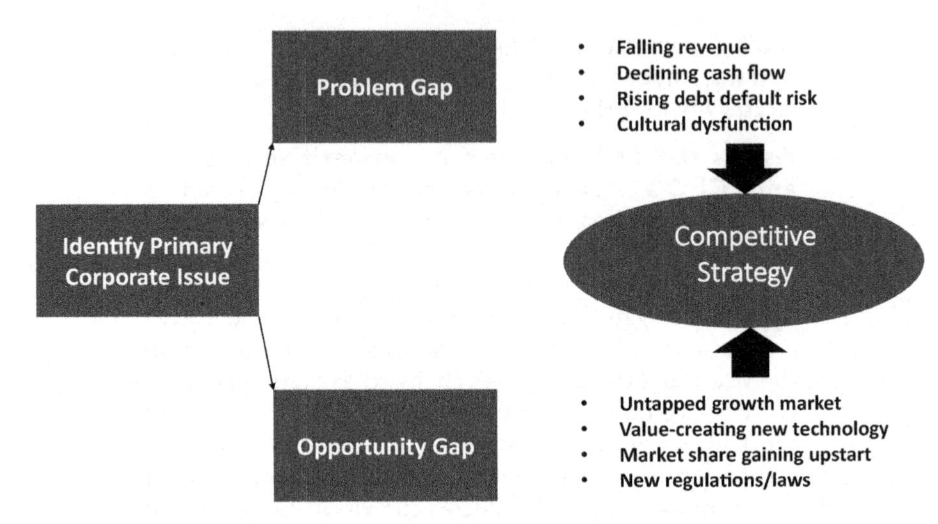

Figure 8-5. Competitive Strategy to Close Problem/Opportunity Gap

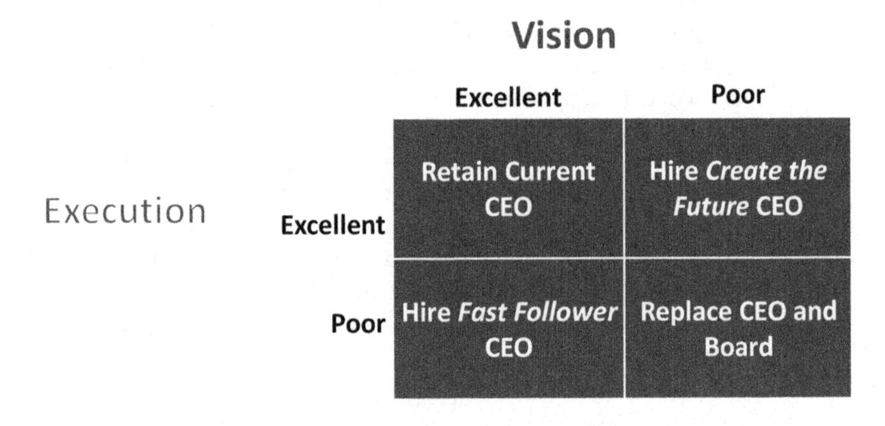

Figure 8-6. Board Assessment of Competitive Strategy and CEO Strategic Mindset

Develop a Competitive Strategy to Close the Problem or Opportunity Gap

The board and the CEO should collaborate to develop a competitive strategy that closes the company's most significant opportunity or problem gap. The relevant industry experience and regular information the CEO shares with the board should enable the board to develop a shared understanding of whether the company's biggest issue is a problem or opportunity gap.

Closing the Problem Gap

Since most boards receive reports on the company's financial condition, if that information is accurate, the board should have an easier time pinpointing a problem gap in the form of rapidly declining revenues, increasingly negative cash flows, or challenges in repaying debt. The board would require a deeper investigation of these troubling financial trends by seeking answers to questions for each of the broad financial challenges. For example,

- Declining revenues
    - If the company competes in different markets, are revenues dropping in all its markets? If not, which ones are suffering the biggest revenue declines?
    - Are revenues in those markets declining due to drop in industry demand, a cut in price, or a loss in market share?
    - If the company is losing market share, which competitors are gaining share and why?
    - Can the company take action to overtake those competitors?
- Increasingly negative cash flows
    - Compared to the company's historical cash flow trends, what factors – for example, declining unit demand, lower prices, higher variable costs, or rising fixed costs – are causing cash flows to become more negative?
- Challenges in repaying debt
    - Does the company's debt repayment schedule reflect the company's most recent borrowings, bank covenants, and interest rates?
    - How likely is the company to continue to be able to meet its payment obligations and fulfill the terms of its debt covenants?
    - If the company is in near term danger of default, what is the status of negotiations with lenders?

One kind of problem gap – cultural dysfunction, for example, sexual harassment or other mistreatment of employees – would most certainly not come from scrutinizing these financial trends. The board might become aware of this class of problems through employee, partner or customer complaints about the company's conduct. Getting to the root cause of such a problem might require the company to investigate – for example, by human resources or legal experts – possibly resulting in changing the CEO or other top executives.

While there is some risk – particularly as I write this four months after the beginning of the Covid-19 pandemic – that an incumbent consumer retailer could be encountering such a problem gap, the means of closing this problem gap are conceptually straightforward, though painful to implement. For example, companies should plan to extend their cash runways by reducing cash outflows – either by selling assets or cutting staff.

Closing the Opportunity Gap

The financial information provided to the board would not suffice to help it identify an opportunity gap. To do that, the board might commission a consulting report that addresses topics such as

- From which industries do we draw our current revenues?
- How are those industries likely to change in the future?
  - Are these industries growing or maturing?
  - Are their profit margins narrowing or widening and why?
  - How are new technologies, evolving customer needs, and upstart business models changing their basis of competition?
- Which new industries could we enter to sustain our growth in the future?
- Of these candidate industries, which ones have the most growth potential?

Answering these questions can help make clear which are the best opportunities for the company. But to identify which of these attractive opportunities on which to focus the company, the board and CEO should investigate questions such as

- Why do the winners in these industries win and why do the losers lose?
- What are the customer purchase criteria (CPC) that buyers use to pick among competing suppliers?
- Compared to competitors, how well does the company satisfy these CPC in the minds of potential customers?

- Does the company have the capabilities needed to keep winning in its current markets and attract new customers in attractive markets where it does not currently compete?
- If not, can the company build or acquire these capabilities?

With answers to these questions in hand, the board should define the company's opportunity gap. Here are some examples of possible opportunity gaps:

- Can the company grow faster than its markets by adopting new technologies?
- Can the company leapfrog a fast-growing competitor by offering customers more value for the price?
- Can the company expand into new, growing markets in countries where it currently does not compete?

The next step should be to ask the CEO to develop and recommend competitive strategies to close the opportunity gap. To that end, the CEO should lead the process of creating a competitive strategy as outlined in Figure 8-7.

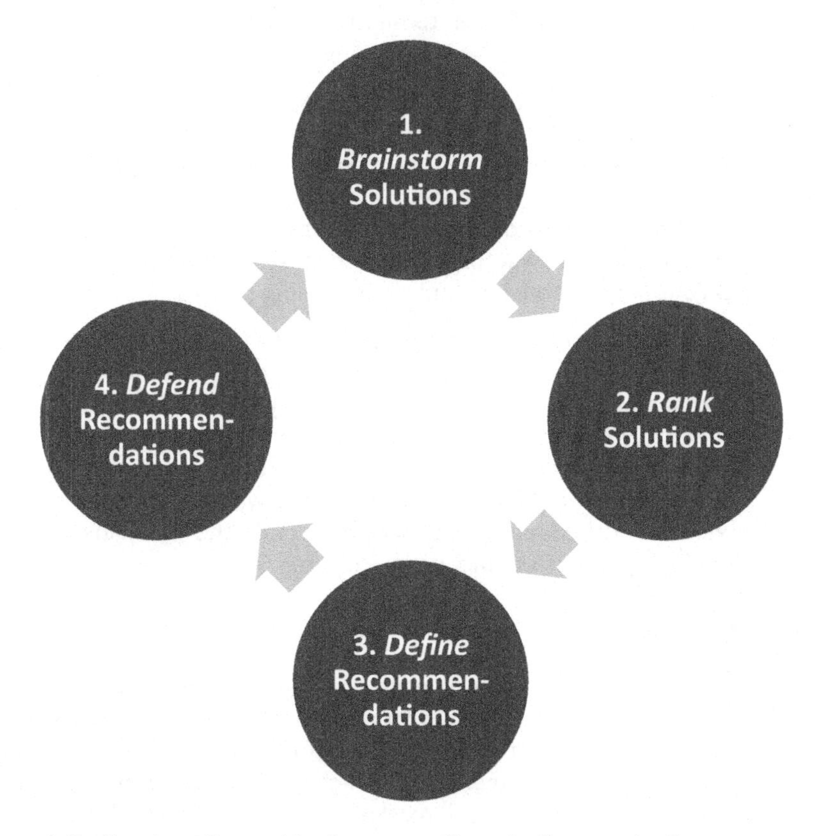

Figure 8-7. Creating a Competitive Strategy to Close the Opportunity Gap

Brainstorm Solutions

The first step in the process of creating a competitive strategy is for the strategy team to brainstorm possible growth vectors using the five dimensions of growth, which include

- **Customer group:** Growth can come from winning more customers from within the company's current target market segment or from a new segment. For example, a business that sells to banks and insurers could grow by selling to more of them or by selling to another segment – such as media and entertainment or retailing.
- **Geography:** Companies can seek additional growth from customers in their current geographies or from new ones. Often companies that have saturated growth opportunities in the United States, for example, will seek to gain market share in China or India.
- **Product:** In addition, companies can grow by developing new products internally or acquiring companies and training their salesforces to sell the acquired company's products.
- **Capabilities:** Companies can grow by using their current capabilities to attack new markets or developing new capabilities which will enable them to tackle those new markets. Netflix developed new capabilities – most notably it produced its own programs and cut its DVD delivery service way back – when it switched from its DVD-by-Mail service to online streaming.
- **Culture:** Of the five dimensions of growth, culture is the most intangible. However, it is worth noting that some companies have cultures that encourage growth more effectively than others. For example, companies that hire and reward people who care about creating value for customers, who think independently, and who collaborate well with other teams and people outside the company tend to grow faster than other cultures.

Rank Solutions

Better solutions result from brainstorming many possibilities. Yet companies generally lack enough capital and talent to implement all the possible solutions. Therefore, leaders must rank the possible solutions – generally based on how much revenue growth they can generate, which is a function of the size of the market and the option's potential market share – in relationship to the investment required. The strategy team can use issue tables which apply common evaluation criteria to each option and score the options from 5, best, to 1, worst, based on a comparison on the following criteria:

- **Market attractiveness:** When comparing options, strategists should gather data on the attractiveness – for example, the size in dollars, growth rate, and average profitability – of the market or markets from which revenues will flow.
- **Competitive advantage:** In addition, strategists should estimate how much each option will increase the company's market share and why. If the company does not currently have a share of the relevant market, the strategy team should make that clear and provide their forecast of how much market share the company can gain in the next five years. The strategy team should also describe why potential customers are likely to prefer the company's product over those of competitors.
- **Net present value:** Net present value is based on forecasting future cash flows over, say, the next years, discounting them into current dollars, and subtracting off the investment required to implement the option. In the issue table, the strategy team should compare the options on the investment required and the NPV.

Define Recommendations

By ranking options using the issue table, the strategy team can pick the one or two best solutions to the core question. Once the team identifies these strategies, it should define its recommendations using the five elements of strategy which include

- **Arenas:** Here, leaders articulate which products they intend to offer to which customer groups as well as how they will distribute the products and in which countries.
- **Vehicles:** Vehicles describe how a company will implement its strategy – either by developing new products, partnering with others, or acquisition.
- **Value proposition:** The value proposition articulates why customers will buy the company's product – by specifying how the company's product prevails over competitors on the customer purchase criteria.

- **Staging:** Staging refers to the sequence of actions the company must undertake to implement the strategy. Staging can be articulated in an implementation plan which lists the actions, accountable managers, deadline, as well as the costs and benefits for each action.
- **Economic logic:** The economic logic describes how the company will earn a profit – either as a low-cost producer, setting the lowest price in the industry, or differentiator, charging the industry's the highest price.

Defend Recommendations

Having articulated their top recommendations, the strategy team must develop a defense of them to present to the company's board of directors. For each recommendation, the strategy team ought to present a more detailed explanation of the following questions:

- **Why is the recommendation's target market attractive?** The strategy team should reiterate the market's size, growth rate, and profitability and explain the factors driving the growth and future profitability of the industries where they are recommending that the company compete.
- **Why will the recommendation boost the company's market share?** The strategy team should reiterate the company's current market share and explain how the recommendation will boost its forecast for the company's market share in five years. The strategy team should also explain why the recommendation will enable the company to prevail over rivals on the most important CPC. Finally, the strategy team should explain the critical activities needed to win on these criteria and why the recommendation will enable the company to prevail on each activity.
- **Why will the recommendation generate a positive NPV?** Here the strategy team should articulate the key assumptions they used in their NPV calculation, including how they calculated the investment required, present their base case NPV, and articulate the robustness of the NPV by describing a sensitivity analysis in which the NPV is recalculated after reducing each of the key assumptions by 10%.

Assess the Fit Between the CEO's Strategic Mindset and the Competitive Strategy

After the CEO presents its recommendations, the board should seek answers to the following questions:

- Will the current CEO's mindset impel or impede the company's ability to grow faster?
- If not, what criteria should the board use to select a new CEO?
- What strategy guidelines should the board give the company's next CEO?

To gain insight into the first question, the board can use the framework outlined in Figure 8-6. If the vision and execution of the CEO's recommendations are sound, the board should seek to retain the current CEO; if the vision is good and the execution needs improvement or vice versa, the board should hire an executive to help bolster the CEO's weaknesses; and if both are poor, the board should replace the CEO. To some extent, the board can assess these questions by evaluating how well the competitive strategy answers the questions outlined in the previous paragraphs on how to create a competitive strategy.

But how will the board assess the CEO's vision and execution? The board can use the framework outlined in Figure 8-8.[10]

Sustainable growth trajectory

Does your company

Solve a problem for which customers are willing to pay a premium price?

Have a clear set of growth vectors from which it will draw revenues?

Raising growth capital

Does your company

Serve customers who will happily refer you to others?

Target very large markets?

Offer enough customer value to gain significant market share?

Field an IPO-ready executive team?

Have the discipline to set and exceed ambitious goals?

Creating growth culture

Does your company

Have clearly articulated values?

Act in ways consistent with its values?

Use its culture to hire, promote, and let people go?

Figure 8-8. Assessing CEO's Vision

Redefining Job Functions

Does your company
- Adapt its organizational structure?
- Limit managerial span of control?
- Give leaders freedom and responsibility?
- Eliminate wasteful functions?

Hiring, Promoting and Letting People Go

Does your company
- Articulate a clear vision and values?
- Promote from within vs. outside hiring?
- Let go those who don't fit future needs?
- Assess cultural fit of outside hires?

Holding People Accountable

Does your company
- Create a performance management team?
- Collaborate to set corporate goals?
- Align functional goals with corporate ones?
- Use system to track progress towards goals?

Coordinating Processes

Does your company
- Create a process management team?
- Engage functions in setting process goals?
- Evaluate process effectiveness?
- Reinvent processes?

Figure 8-9. Assessing CEO's Execution

To assess the strength of the CEO's vision, the board can evaluate the quality of the three topics depicted in Figure 8-8:

- **Growth trajectory:** Based on customer feedback and analysis of competitor strategies, the board can evaluate whether the company is solving a problem that customers perceive as painful; whether its solution to the problem offers more benefits for the price than do competing products; and whether the company has a compelling set of future growth vectors – for example, customer groups, geographies, and products in which it will invest to achieve continued growth.
- **Growth capital raising:** For a publicly traded company – unless it is suffering severe cash flow problems – raising growth capital is less time-consuming than for a startup. To persuade the board to allocate capital to implement the growth trajectory, the CEO must make a fact-based case that the vision will enable the company to gain a large enough share of large new market opportunities to earn an attractive return on the deployed capital.
- **Culture of growth:** To attract and motivate the top-rate talent required to achieve the desired revenue growth, the CEO must create a culture of growth. The key elements of such a culture are a corporate mission that attracts talent and a set of action-backed values that motivate the talent to listen to customers and respond to their evolving needs by providing them products that industry-prevailing value to customers.

To assess the strength of the CEO's execution skills, the board can evaluate the quality of the four topics depicted in Figure 8-9:

- **Redefining job functions:** A company must employ people with the skills needed to perform the critical activities required to execute it. For example, if an incumbent retailer decides to boost its online revenues, it must employ a team that can deploy the technology and business processes needed to purchase a wide variety of inventories, display the options to consumers visiting online or via an app, enable customers to place their orders, fulfill the orders accurately and on time, and respond to customer questions to assure that they are satisfied. One test of a CEO's ability to execute their vision is whether these functions are clearly defined in the company's organization structure.
- **Hiring, promoting, and letting people go:** With the aid of a clearly defined and widely understood growth culture, a CEO ought to make sure that the best possible talent occupies the roles redefined to enable the company to execute the vision. Along with filling these critical jobs with the best talent, the CEO must attract new talent to fill roles left open by promotions and departures of those who do not fit with the company's culture or cannot do the work required of them.
- **Holding people accountable:** With the right people in the right jobs, the CEO must hold them accountable for achieving specific business objectives for their functions that will, when aggregated, enable the company to grow faster and realize the CEO's vision. To do that, people in each function ought to set their own goals – in coordination with the leadership team – to assure that everyone in the company is "rowing" toward the same goal. Setting the right goals and tracking their achievement will strengthen the execution of the CEO's vision.
- **Coordinating processes:** To avoid wasting effort in pursuit of these goals and boost efficiency of execution, the company ought to set up processes – such as new product development, order fulfillment, and customer success – that cut across functions. Such coordination can help avoid missteps and reduce the number of repeated steps performed by different functions. Coordinating the processes can also enable the company to become aware of and adapt more quickly to unpleasant surprises.

By assessing the vision and execution of the CEO's competitive strategy in this way, the board can assess whether the current CEO's strategic mindset fits what the company needs for future success. If the board determines that the CEO's competitive strategy will close the problem or opportunity gap and that the vision and its execution are strong, then the CEO's strategic mindset is a good fit. If the board concludes that the CEO's competitive strategy does not close the problem or opportunity gap, then a new CEO should be hired – and the board will likely need to decide whether to pick a successor with a *Create the Future* or *Fast Follower* mindset to come up with a better strategy. If the board concludes that the competitive strategy is sound – but the CEO's vision or execution is weak, then the board might consider bringing in a co-CEO or chief operating officer with a mindset that complements the current CEO.

Conclusion

For decades, a dominant narrative in business has been the feisty upstart knocking down the lumbering giant. The idea behind this story was that all the resources the large incumbents controlled were impeding their ability to sense changes in customer needs, develop or deploy new technology, and invent new business models that customers would find more compelling. Through the 18 case studies of *Create the Future, Fast Follower*, and *Head in the Sand* strategic mindsets, we have seen that this David vs. Goliath narrative is not immutable. Indeed, in some of the book's case studies – such as Best Buy in consumer electronics, *The New York Times* in news, and Walmart in groceries – a *Fast Follower* mindset was able to overcome a Goliath's inherent inertia and mobilize the company's strengths into a much stronger competitive position that spurred faster revenue growth, happier employees, more satisfied customers, and richer shareholders. By engaging in a fact-based dialogue over strategy and execution between the CEO and an independent board, a company can assure that there is a tight fit between the strategic mindset of the CEO and the competitive strategy needed to close the company's opportunity or problem gap.

APPENDIX

A

Notes

Chapter 1: Introduction

[1] Day One Staff, "2016 Letter to Shareholders," *Amazon.com*, April 17, 2017. https://blog.aboutamazon.com/company-news/2016-letter-to-shareholders.

[2] Peter Cohan, "Wharton, MIT Professors See Upside At Nordstrom, Kohl's, And Target," *Forbes*, September 26, 2019. https://www.forbes.com/sites/petercohan/2019/09/26/wharton-mit-professors-see-upside-at-nordstrom-kohls-and-target/#4ac67e4a14d7.

[3] Ibid.

[4] Ibid.

[5] Ibid.

[6] Ibid.

[7] Suzanne Kapner, "Amazon Didn't Cripple Bed Bath & Beyond. Its Own Leaders Did.," *Wall Street Journal*, June 2, 2019. https://www.wsj.com/articles/amazon-didnt-cripple-bed-bath-beyond-its-own-leaders-did-11559467800.

[8] Peter Cohan, "With Shares Up 93%, Target's Turnaround Suggests Powerful Investment Strategy," *Forbes*, October 18, 2019. https://www.forbes.com/sites/petercohan/2019/10/18/with-shares-up-93-targets-turnaround-suggests-powerful-investment-strategy/#5d58f675251d.

[9] Ibid.

[10] Ibid.

P. S. Cohan, *Goliath Strikes Back*, https://doi.org/10.1007/978-1-4842-6519-2

[11] Ibid.

[12] Ibid.

Chapter 2: Consumer Electronics

[1] "Consumer Electronics Stores," *IBISWorld*, accessed November 15, 2019. https://www.ibisworld.com/united-states/market-research-reports/consumer-electronics-stores-industry/.

[2] Ibid.

[3] Ibid.

[4] Ibid.

[5] Ibid.

[6] Cecilia Fernandez, "Consumer Electronics Stores in the US," *IBISWorld*, July 2020. https://www.ibisworld.com/united-states/market-research-reports/consumer-electronics-stores-industry/.

[7] Teresa Rivas, "Best Buy May End Coronavirus Pandemic as a 'Winner in Retail'," *Barron's*, May 18, 2020. https://www.barrons.com/articles/best-buy-sales-earnings-ugrade-outlook-coronavirus-pandemic-51589815068.

[8] Jeremy C. Owens, "Best Buy says sales are better during pandemic, stock heads toward all-time high," *MarketWatch*, July 21, 2020. https://www.marketwatch.com/story/best-buy-says-sales-are-better-during-pandemic-stock-heads-toward-all-time-high-2020-07-21.

[9] Daphne Howland, "Amazon beats Best Buy as top electronics retailer," *Retail Dive*, April 17, 2018. https://www.retaildive.com/news/amazon-beats-best-buy-as-top-electronics-retailer/521505/.

[10] Rob Stott, "The Rich Get Richer in Dealerscope's 2019 Top 101 CE Retailers," *Dealerscope*, April 16, 2019. https://www.dealerscope.com/article/the-rich-get-richer-in-dealerscopes-2019-top-101-ce-retailers/.

[11] Daphne Howland, *Retail Dive*.

[12] Daphne Howland, *Retail Dive*.

[13] Derek Haines, "Kindle Sales – The E-Reader Device Is Dying A Rapid Death," *Just Publishing Advice*, November 17, 2019. https://justpublishingadvice.com/the-e-reader-device-is-dying-a-rapid-death/.

[14] Adam Levy, "Amazon's Alexa Is a Multibillion-Dollar Business," *The Motley Fool*, September 28, 2019. https://www.fool.com/investing/2019/09/28/amazons-alexa-is-a-multibillion-dollar-business.aspx.

[15] Rebecca Ungarino, "Amazon's Alexa could be a $19 billion business by 2021, RBC says (AMZN)," *Markets Insider*, December 21, 2018. https://markets.businessinsider.com/news/stocks/amazon-stock-price-alexa-19-billion-business-rbc-says-2018-12-1027829391.

[16] Nick Chasinov, "How Amazon Became The #1 Consumer Electronics Retailer," *Technicks*, April 24, 2018. https://blog.teknicks.com/how-amazon-became-the-1-consumer-electronics-retailer#.XcguYTbsa1s.

[17] Peter Cohan, "Value Leadership: 7 Principles That Drive Corporate Value in Any Economy," *Wiley*, 2003.

[18] Peter Cohan, "The CEO Who Saved Best Buy from Ruin Says Creating Meaning at Work Was Key to His Success," *Inc.* November 20, 2019. https://www.inc.com/peter-cohan/the-ceo-who-saved-best-buy-from-ruin-says-creating-meaning-at-work-was-key-to-his-success.html.

[19] Ibid.

[20] "CNBC TRANSCRIPT: CNBC'S COURTNEY REAGAN INTERVIEWS BEST BUY EXECUTIVE CHAIRMAN AND FORMER CEO HUBERT JOLY FROM THE CNBC EVOLVE CONFERENCE IN NYC TODAY," *CNBC*, June 19, 2019. https://www.nbcumv.com/news/cnbc-transcript-cnbc%E2%80%99s-courtney-reagan-interviews-best-buy-executive-chairman-and-former-ceo.

[21] Burl Gilyard, "2018 Person of the Year: Hubert Joly," *TCB Magazine*, November 27, 2018. http://tcbmag.com/honors/articles/2018/2018-person-of-the-year-hubert-joly.

[22] Jeff Spross, "How Best Buy survived the retail apocalypse," *The Week*, October 22, 2018. https://theweek.com/articles/802800/how-best-buy-survived-retail-apocalypse.

[23] Marianne Gérard, "Hubert Joly (Best Buy): "Managing means creating meaning," *HEC stories*, July 18, 2019. https://hecstories.fr/en/hubert-joly-best-buy-managing-means-creating-meaning/.

[24] Burl Gilyard, *TCB Magazine*.

[25] Maxwell Wessel, "It's All About Mindset — Hubert Joly, CEO Best Buy," *Medium*, March 7, 2019. https://medium.com/the-industrialist-s-dilemma/its-all-about-mindset-hubert-joly-ceo-best-buy-aac74056d075.

[26] "Circuit City 2008 10K," *sec.gov*, April 28, 2008. https://www.sec.gov/Archives/edgar/data/104599/000119312508093063/d10k.htm.

[27] "Circuit City files for bankruptcy protection," *Reuters*, November 10, 2008. https://www.reuters.com/article/us-circuitcity-idUSTRE4A936V20081110.

[28] Anita Hamilton, "Why Circuit City Busted, While Best Buy Boomed," *Time*, November 11, 2008. http://content.time.com/time/business/article/0,8599,1858079,00.html.

[29] Louis Llovio, "Former Circuit City CEO and chairman talks of company's demise, *Richmond Times Dispatch*, October 18, 2012. https://www.richmond.com/business/former-circuit-city-ceo-and-chairman-talks-of-company-s/article_8e219f23-721b-5a54-b6c2-3e1b35536557.html.

[30] Anita Hamilton, *Time*.

[31] Phil Schoonover, LinkedIn profile, accessed November 24, 2019. https://www.linkedin.com/in/philipschoonover/.

[32] Jessie Romero, "The Rise and Fall of Circuit City," *Econ Focus*. Third Quarter, 2013. https://www.richmondfed.org/~/media/richmondfedorg/publications/research/econ_focus/2013/q3/pdf/economic_history.pdf.

[33] Louis Llovio. *Richmond Times Dispatch*.

Chapter 3: Video Entertainment

[1] Ken Auletta, "Outside the Box: Netflix and the future of television," *New Yorker*, January 26, 2014. https://www.newyorker.com/magazine/2014/02/03/outside-the-box-2.

[2] Amy Watson, "OTT revenue worldwide from 2010 to 2024," *Statista*, December 4, 2019. https://www.statista.com/statistics/260179/over-the-top-revenue-worldwide./.

[3] Jim Nail and Andrew Hogan, "The Forrester Streaming Media Wave: US Apps, Q4 2019," *Forrester Research*, October 28, 2019. https://www.forrester.com/report/The+Forrester+Streaming+Media+Wave+US+Apps+Q4+2019/-/E-RES146298.

[4] Benjamin Wallace, "Is Anyone Watching Quibi?," *Vulture*, July 6, 2020. https://www.vulture.com/2020/07/is-anyone-watching-quibi.html.

[5] "Media Consumption in the Age of COVID-19," *J.P. Morgan*, May 1, 2020. https://www.jpmorgan.com/global/research/media-consumption.

[6] Daniel Sparks, "Netflix's Subscribers May Have Hit 166 Million in 2019," *The Motley Fool*, January 3, 2020. https://www.fool.com/investing/2020/01/03/netflixs-subscribers-may-have-hit-166-million-in-2.aspx.

[7] Peter Cohan, "5 Reasons Not To Bet Netflix Will Soar Another 4,100% By 2030," *Forbes*, January 2, 2020. https://www.forbes.com/sites/petercohan/2020/01/02/5-reasons-not-to-bet-netflix-will-soar-another-4100-by-2030/#1a2e00476bd6.

[8] Bill Snyder, "Another Netflix Disruption: A Transparent Board," *Stanford Graduate School of Business*, May 2, 2018. https://www.gsb.stanford.edu/insights/another-netflix-disruption-transparent-board.

[9] Anne Quito, "Netflix CEO Reed Hastings is the un-decider," *Quartz*, April 19, 2018. https://qz.com/work/1254183/netflix-ceo-reed-hastings-expounds-on-the-netflix-culture-deck-at-ted-2018/.

[10] Ken Auletta, *New Yorker*.

[11] Miguel Helft, "Netflix to Deliver Movies to the PC," *New York Times*, January 16, 2007. https://www.nytimes.com/2007/01/16/technology/16netflix.html.

[12] Ken Auletta, *New Yorker*.

[13] Todd Spangler, "Netflix, YouTube Share of U.S. Viewing Time Projected to Drop in 2020," *Variety*, December 3, 2019. https://variety.com/2019/digital/news/netflix-youtube-share-us-video-viewing-drop-1203421385/.

[14] Peter Cohan, *Forbes*.

[15] "How streaming started," *Thinknum*, accessed December 27, 2019. https://media.thinknum.com/articles/a-brief-history-of-video-streaming-by-the-numbers/.

[16] Ken Auletta, *New Yorker*.

[17] Edmund Lee, "Disney has struck a deal with Comcast that will give it full control of the streaming service," *New York Times*, May 14, 2019. https://www.nytimes.com/2019/05/14/business/media/disney-hulu-comcast.html.

[18] Amol Sharma and Joe Flint, "The Great Streaming Battle Is Here. No One Is Safe. Netflix, the current heavyweight, is in for a fight as Disney, Apple, AT&T and Comcast enter the ring this year and next," *Wall Street Journal*, November 9, 2019. https://www.wsj.com/articles/the-great-streaming-battle-is-here-no-one-is-safe-11573272000?mod=article_inline.

[19] Cortney Moore, "Hulu and the 5 things that set it apart from other streaming giants," *Fox Business*, September 30, 2019. https://www.foxbusiness.com/technology/5-things-to-know-about-hulu.

[20] Ryan Faughnder, "Disney's Hulu is raising prices for live TV as costs escalate," *Los Angeles Times*, November 15, 2019. https://www.latimes.com/entertainment-arts/business/story/2019-11-15/hulu-raises-price-for-live-tv.

[21] "Compaq to buy DEC," *CNNMoney*, January 26, 1998. https://money.cnn.com/1998/01/26/technology/compaq/.

[22] Jeanine Poggi, "Blockbuster's Rise and Fall: The Long, Rewinding Road," *TheStreet.com*, September 23, 2010. https://www.thestreet.com/investing/stocks/the-rise-and-fall-of-blockbuster-the-long-rewinding-road-10867574.

[23] Ibid.

[24] Ibid.

[25] Ken Auletta, *New Yorker.*

[26] Jeanine Poggi, *TheStreet.com.*

[27] Jeanine Poggi, *TheStreet.com.*

[28] Michael de la Merced, "Blockbuster, Hoping to Reinvent Itself, Files for Bankruptcy," *New York Times*, September 23, 2010. https://www.nytimes.com/2010/09/24/business/24blockbuster.html.

[29] "Blockbuster Weakened: Peter Cohan on the Video Giant's Decline," *Drucker Institute*, October 4, 2010. https://www.drucker.institute/thedx/blockbuster-weakened-peter-cohan-on-the-video-giants-decline/.

Chapter 4: Newspapers

[1] Devin McGinley, "Newspaper Publishing in the US," *IBISWorld*, December 2019. https://www.ibisworld.com/united-states/market-research-reports/newspaper-publishing-industry/.

[2] Keach Hagey, Lukas I. Alpert and Yaryna Serkez, "In News Industry, a Stark Divide Between Haves and Have-Nots," *Wall Street Journal*, May 4, 2019. https://www.wsj.com/graphics/local-newspapers-stark-divide/.

[3] Clayton M. Christensen, David Skok, James Allworth, "Breaking News," *Nieman Reports*, September 15, 2012. https://niemanreports.org/articles/breaking-news/.

[4] Keach Hagey, Lukas I. Alpert and Yaryna Serkez, *Wall Street Journal.*

[5] Peter Cohan, "Dead Tree Industry: New York Times, Google, And Hedge Fund Harvesters," *Forbes*, February 11, 2020. https://www.forbes.com/sites/petercohan/2020/02/11/dead-tree-industry-new-york-times-google-and-hedge-fund-harvesters/#e67ff986bf65.

[6] Devin McGinley, *IBISWorld.*

[7] Peter Cohan, *Forbes.*

[8] Devin McGinley, *IBISWorld*.

[9] Keach Hagey, Lukas I. Alpert and Yaryna Serkez, *Wall Street Journal*.

[10] Keach Hagey, Lukas I. Alpert and Yaryna Serkez, *Wall Street Journal*.

[11] Peter Cohan, *Forbes*.

[12] Nicole Friedman, "Warren Buffett Is Giving Up on Newspapers," *Wall Street Journal*, January 29, 2020. https://www.wsj.com/articles/warren-buffett-is-giving-up-on-newspapers-11580301637.

[13] Sam Ro, "Warren Buffett says the newspaper business is 'toast'," *Yahoo Finance*, April 29, 2019. https://finance.yahoo.com/news/warren-buffett-newspapers-are-toast-exclusive-133720666.html.

[14] Sarah Barry James, "Newspapers fighting for survival as COVID-19 ravages ad spending," *S&P Global*, April 27, 2020. https://www.spglobal.com/marketintelligence/en/news-insights/latest-news-headlines/newspapers-fighting-for-survival-as-covid-19-ravages-ad-spending-58306183.

[15] Mary Bellis, "The History of Google and How It Was Invented," *Thoughtco*, January 29, 2020. https://www.thoughtco.com/who-invented-google-1991852.

[16] "Alphabet A', Morningstar, accessed February 21, 2012. https://www.morningstar.com/stocks/xnas/googl/quote.

[17] Tom Johansmeyer, "Advertising History Is Made — Web Ads Overtook Newspaper Ads in 2010," *AdWeek*, December 20, 2010. https://www.adweek.com/digital/online-overtakes-newspaper-ad-revenue-so-does-google/.

[18] Alec Stapp, "Google And Facebook Didn't Kill Newspapers: The Internet Did," *Techdirt*, October 25, 2019. https://www.techdirt.com/articles/20191024/13182743257/google-facebook-didnt-kill-newspapers-internet-did.shtml.

[19] "Rather than paying the maximum bid for the keyword, the winning bidder pays the lowest amount required to exceed the next highest bid. "Google AdWords Auction – A Second Price Sealed-Bid Auction," *Cornell University*, accessed February 22, 2020. https://blogs.cornell.edu/info2040/2012/10/27/google-adwords-auction-a-second-price-sealed-bid-auction/.

[20] Will Oremus, "Google's Big Break," *Slate*, October 13, 2013. https://slate.com/business/2013/10/googles-big-break-how-bill-gross-goto-com-inspired-the-adwords-business-model.html.

[21] Patience Haggin and Kara Dapen, "Google's Ad Dominance Explained in Three Charts," *Wall Street Journal*, June 17, 2019. https://www.wsj.com/articles/why-googles-advertising-dominance-is-drawing-antitrust-scrutiny-11560763800.

[22] Danielle Abril, "Google's annual ad sales are expected to decline for first time in 16 years," *Fortune*, June 22, 2020. https://fortune.com/2020/06/22/google-ad-revenues-to-drop-coronavirus-covid-19/.

[23] "New York Times CEO Mark Thompson on growing newspaper company by billions during Trump's 'fake news' era,' *CNBC*, June 19, 2019. https://www.cnbc.com/2019/06/19/new-york-times-ceo-on-how-newspaper-grew-300percent-amid-fake-news-bashing.html.

[24] "The New York Times Now Gets More Revenue from Subscribers Than Advertisers," *Agence France Presse*, February 8, 2013. https://www.businessinsider.com/the-new-york-times-now-gets-more-revenue-from-subscribers-than-advertisers-2013-2.

[25] Marc Tracy, "The New York Times Tops 5 Million Subscriptions as Ads Decline," *New York Times*, February 6, 2020. https://www.nytimes.com/2020/02/06/business/new-york-times-earning.html.

[26] Astrid Stawiarz, "CNBC: Mark Thompson at CNBC Evolve," *CNBC*, June 19, 2019. https://www.cnbc.com/2019/06/19/new-york-times-ceo-on-how-newspaper-grew-300percent-amid-fake-news-bashing.html.

[27] Vineet Kumar, Bharat Anand, Sunil Gupta, Felix Oberholzer-Gee, "The New York Times Paywall," *Harvard Business School*, January 31, 2013. https://papers.ssrn.com/sol3/papers.cfm?abstract_id=2053220.

[28] Marc Tracy, *New York Times*.

[29] Tali Arbel, "NY Times publisher's 4Q profit grows as it adds subscribers," *Associated Press*, February 6, 2020. https://www.seattletimes.com/business/ny-times-publishers-4q-profit-grows-as-it-adds-subscribers/.

[30] Peter Cohan, *Forbes*.

[31] Sara Jerde, "Even as Ad Revenue Drops, New York Times Sets Subscription Records," *AdWeek*, May 6, 2020. https://www.adweek.com/digital/even-as-ad-revenue-drops-new-york-times-sets-subscription-records/.

[32] "The Times Mirror Publishing Co., owner of major newspapers...," *UPI Archives*, October 23, 1980. https://www.upi.com/Archives/1980/10/23/The-Times-Mirror-Publishing-Co-owner-of-major-newspapers/7844341121600/.

[33] Geraldine Fabrikant, "Texan Is Buying His 29th Daily, The Denver Post," *The New York Times*, September 15, 1987. https://www.nytimes.com/1987/09/15/business/texan-is-buying-his-29th-daily-the-denver-post.html.

[34] Aldo Svaldi, "Texas newspaperman put his brand on The Denver Post — and saved it from extinction," *Denver Post*, October 15, 2017. https://www.denverpost.com/2017/10/15/dean-singleton-the-denver-post/.

[35] Ibid.

[36] Joe Pompeo, "The Hedge Fund Vampire That Bleeds Newspapers Dry Now Has the Chicago Tribune by the Throat," *Vanity Fair*, February 5, 2020. https://www.vanityfair.com/news/2020/02/hedge-fund-vampire-alden-global-capital-that-bleeds-newspapers-dry-has-chicago-tribune-by-the-throat.

[37] Jonathan O'Connell and Emma Brown, "A hedge fund's 'mercenary' strategy: Buy newspapers, slash jobs, sell the buildings," *Washington Post*, February 11, 2019. https://www.washingtonpost.com/business/economy/a-hedge-funds-mercenary-strategy-buy-newspapers-slash-jobs-sell-the-buildings/2019/02/11/f2c0c78a-1f59-11e9-8e21-59a09ff1e2a1_story.html.

[38] Rick Edmonds, "Is Alden the archvillain crushing local news? It's a little more complicated," *Poynter*, February 20, 2020. https://www.poynter.org/business-work/2020/is-alden-the-archvillain-crushing-local-news-its-a-little-more-complicated/.

Chapter 5: Groceries

[1] Cecilia Fernandez, "Supermarkets & Grocery Stores in the US," *IBISWorld*, December 2019. https://www.ibisworld.com/united-states/market-research-reports/supermarkets-grocery-stores-industry/.

[2] Ibid.

[3] Jaewon Kang, "Specialty Grocers Lose Their Edge," Wall Street Journal, March 1, 2020. https://www.wsj.com/articles/upscale-specialty-grocers-lose-their-edge-11583058601.

[4] Cecilia Fernandez, *IBISWorld*.

[5] Cecilia Fernandez, "Supermarkets & Grocery Stores in the US," IBISWorld, May 2020. https://www.ibisworld.com/united-states/market-research-reports/supermarkets-grocery-stores-industry/.

[6] Ibid.

[7] Alison Griswold, "Why Jeff Bezos is obsessed with groceries," *Quartz*, June 16, 2017. https://qz.com/1008027/why-did-amazon-buy-whole-foods-ceo-jeff-bezos-is-obsessed-with-groceries/.

[8] Alistair Barr, "From the ashes of Webvan, Amazon builds a grocery business," *Reuters*, June 18, 2013. https://www.reuters.com/article/net-us-amazon-webvan/from-the-ashes-of-webvan-amazon-builds-a-grocery-business-idUSBRE95H1CC20130618.

[9] James F. Peltz, "Amazon plans new grocery store in L.A. as it thinks about how to conquer the industry," November 11, 2019. *Los Angeles Times*, https://www.latimes.com/business/story/2019-11-11/amazon-to-open-new-grocery-store-in-los-angeles-2020.

[10] Spencer Soper and Olivia Zaleski, "Inside Amazon's Battle to Break Into the $800 Billion Grocery Market," *Bloomberg*, March 20, 2017. https://www.bloomberg.com/news/features/2017-03-20/inside-amazon-s-battle-to-break-into-the-800-billion-grocery-market.

[11] Alison Griswold, *Quartz*.

[12] Spencer Soper and Olivia Zaleski, *Bloomberg*.

[13] Alison Griswold, *Quartz*.

[14] Spencer Soper and Olivia Zaleski, *Bloomberg*.

[15] Spencer Soper and Olivia Zaleski, *Bloomberg*.

[16] Sebastian Herrera and Aaron Tilley, "Amazon Opens Cashierless Supermarket in Latest Push to Sell Food," *Wall Street Journal*, February 25, 2020. https://www.wsj.com/articles/amazon-opens-cashierless-supermarket-in-latest-push-to-sell-food-11582617660.

[17] Cecilia Fernandez, *IBISWorld*.

[18] Andria Cheng, "Two Years After Amazon Deal, Whole Foods Is Still Working to Shed Its 'Whole Paycheck' Image," *Forbes*, August 28, 2019. https://www.forbes.com/sites/andriacheng/2019/08/28/two-years-under-amazon-whole-foods-still-has-its-work-cut-out-to-erase-the-whole-paycheck-image/#5db434594227.

[19] Jay Greene, "Amazon pushes further into grocery business with new Los Angeles store," *Washington Post*, November 11, 2019. https://www.washingtonpost.com/technology/2019/11/11/amazon-pushes-farther-into-grocery-business-with-new-los-angeles-store/.

[20] Cecilia Fernandez, *IBISWorld*.

[21] Marc Bain, "Covid-19 is helping Walmart make up ground against Amazon," *Quartz*, May 19, 2020. https://qz.com/1858747/covid-19-is-helping-walmart-make-up-ground-against-amazon/.

[22] Lauren Thomas, "Walmart is a grocery powerhouse ... and it still has room to run," *CNBC*, November 14, 2019. https://www.cnbc.com/2019/11/14/walmart-is-a-grocery-powerhouse-and-it-still-has-room-to-run.html.

[23] Cecilia Fernandez, *IBISWorld*.

[24] Meredith Lepore, "Here's How Walmart Became The #1 Grocery Store in The Country," *Business Insider*, February 2011. https://www.businessinsider.com/walmart-biggest-supermarket-2011-2.

[25] Hank Gilman, "The Most Underrated CEO Ever," *Fortune*, April 5, 2004. https://archive.fortune.com/magazines/fortune/fortune_archive/2004/04/05/366366/index.htm.

[26] "CNBC TRANSCRIPT: CNBC'S BECKY QUICK INTERVIEWS WALMART CEO DOUG MCMILLON FROM THE CNBC EVOLVE CONFERENCE IN LOS ANGELES TODAY," *CNBC*, November 19, 2019. https://www.nbcumv.com/news/cnbc-transcript-cnbc%E2%80%99s-becky-quick-interviews-walmart-ceo-doug-mcmillon-cnbc-evolve-conference.

[27] Courtney Reagan, "Walmart will now put groceries right in your fridge, starting in 3 cities Tuesday," *CNBC*, October 15, 2019. https://www.cnbc.com/2019/10/15/walmart-will-now-put-groceries-right-in-your-fridge-starting-in-3-cities-tuesday.html.

[28] Becky Quick, *CNBC*.

[29] Sarah Nassauer, "Walmart Sales Surge as Coronavirus Drives Americans to Stockpile," *Wall Street Journal*, May 19, 2020. https://www.wsj.com/articles/walmart-sales-surge-as-coronavirus-drives-americans-to-stockpile-11589888464.

[30] Tyler Durden, "Why America's First National Supermarket Chain Just Filed for Bankruptcy, Again," *ZeroHedge*, July 20, 2015. https://www.zerohedge.com/news/2015-07-20/why-americas-first-national-supermarket-chain-just-filed-bankruptcy-again-spoiler-al.

[31] Email to author from Marc Levinson, author of *The Great A&P and the Struggle for Small Business in America* (2012), March 1, 2020.

[32] Marc Levinson, "Don't Grieve for the Great A&P," *Harvard Business Review*, January 30, 2012. https://hbr.org/2012/01/dont-grieve-for-the-great-ap.

[33] Ibid.

[34] Levinson email.

[35] Brian Harris, "What Went Wrong With A&P?" *Blog.Zenput*, accessed March 26, 2020. https://blog.zenput.com/what-went-wrong-with-ap.

[36] Tyler Durden, *ZeroHedge*.

[37] Levinson email.

[38] Durden, Ibid.

[39] Tyler Durden, *ZeroHedge*.

[40] Annie Gasparro and Joseph Checkler, "A&P Bankruptcy Filing Indicates Likely Demise," *Wall Street Journal*, July 20, 2015. https://www.wsj.com/articles/a-p-files-for-chapter-11-bankruptcy-1437391572.

[41] Levinson email.

Chapter 6: Furniture

[1] Nafia Islam, "Online Household Furniture Sales," *IBISWorld*, December 2018. https://my-ibisworld-com.ezproxy.babson.edu/us/en/industry-specialized/od5076/industry-at-a-glance.

[2] Claire O'Connor, "Furniture Stores in the US," *IBISWorld*, December 2019. https://my-ibisworld-com.ezproxy.babson.edu/us/en/industry/44211/industry-at-a-glance.

[3] Claire O'Connor, *IBISWorld*.

[4] Nafia Islam, *IBISWorld*.

[5] "How Kamprad Became King of IKEA," *Sweden.se/business*, accessed April 11, 2020. https://sweden.se/business/ingvar-kamprad-founder-of-ikea/.

[6] Claire O'Connor, *IBISWorld*.

[7] Robert D. McFadden, "Ingvar Kamprad, Founder of Ikea and Creator of a Global Empire, Dies at 91," *New York Times*, January 28, 2018. https://www.nytimes.com/2018/01/28/obituaries/ingvar-kamprad-dies.html.

[8] Claire O'Connor, *IBISWorld*.

[9] Arlene Hirst, "How Ikea Became America's Furniture-Selling Powerhouse," *Curbed*, October 8, 2014. https://www.curbed.com/2014/10/8/10038294/how-ikea-became-americas-furnitureselling-powerhouse.

[10] Claire O'Connor, *IBISWorld*.

[11] Catherine Clifford, "Meatballs and DIY bookcases: The psychology behind Ikea's iconic success, *CNBC*, October 5, 2019. https://www.cnbc.com/2019/10/05/psychology-behind-ikeas-huge-success.html.

[12] Stephanie Mehta, "Exclusive: Ikea's CEO says the company is testing 'everything you can dream of'," *Fast Company*, January 6, 2020. https://www.fastcompany.com/90501603/masks-prevent-the-spread-of-Covid-19-landmark-analysis-of-64-studies-finds.

[13] Evan Nicole Brown, "Ikea's new digital strategy engages users where they are: At home," *Fast Company*, April 3, 2020. https://www.fastcompany.com/90485649/ikeas-new-digital-strategy-engages-users-where-they-are-at-home.

[14] Nafia Islam, *IBISWorld*.

[15] Larry Kim, "Get to Know Wayfair's Founder: 10 Facts About Niraj Shah," *Inc.*, June 25, 2019. https://www.inc.com/larry-kim/get-to-know-wayfairs-founder-10-facts-about-niraj-shah.html.

[16] Peter Cohan, "Why Wayfair Won and Furniture.com Flopped," *Inc.*, May 11, 2017. https://www.inc.com/peter-cohan/why-wayfair-won-and-furniturecom-flopped.html.

[17] Cheryl Wischhover, "Wayfair, the internet's massive online furniture store, explained," Vox, August 28, 2019. https://www.vox.com/2019/8/28/20833645/wayfair-many-brands-websites.

[18] Justine Hofherr, "How Wayfair's CEO hires employees, builds office culture and unwinds at home," *Boston Globe*, May 6, 2016. https://www.boston.com/news/jobs/2016/05/06/wayfair-ceo-niraj-shah.

[19] "Exclusive Interview with Wayfair CEO & eCommerce Entrepreneur Niraj Shah," *Alister & Paine*, February 18, 2013. https://alisterpaine.com/2013/02/18/exclusive-interview-with-wayfair-ceo-ecommerce-entrepreneur-niraj-shah/.

[20] "Wayfair 2019 10K," sec.gov, February 18, 2019. https://www.sec.gov/ix?doc=/Archives/edgar/data/1616707/000161670720000025/a2019-12x31form10xk.htm.

[21] Chris Sweeney, "Inside Wayfair's Identity Crisis," *Boston Magazine*, October 1, 2019. https://www.bostonmagazine.com/news/2019/10/01/inside-wayfair/.

[22] Peter Cohan, "Plummeting Machete: Down 53%, Avoid Wayfair Stock," *Forbes*, February 2, 2020. https://www.forbes.com/sites/petercohan/2020/02/14/plummeting-machete-down-53-avoid-wayfair-stock/#16fe7b6832aa.

[23] Chris Sweeney, *Boston Magazine*.

[24] Chris Sweeney, *Boston Magazine*.

[25] Peter Cohan, *Forbes*.

[26] Janet Freund, "Wayfair Surges Most Ever, Buoyed by Shopping Spree on Furniture," *Bloomberg*, April 6, 2020. https://www.bloomberg.com/news/articles/2020-04-06/wayfair-surges-most-ever-amid-online-furniture-spending-spree.

[27] Janelle Nanos, "More job cuts hit Boston's tech sector as coronavirus effects spread," *Boston Globe*, April 8, 2020. https://www.bostonglobe.com/2020/04/08/nation/more-job-cuts-hit-bostons-tech-sector-coronavirus-effects-spread/?event=event12.

[28] Peter Cohan, "How COVID-19 Is Boosting Wayfair Stock," *Forbes*, April 21, 2020. https://www.forbes.com/sites/petercohan/2020/04/21/how-Covid-19-is-boosting-wayfair-stock/#46db05707b11.

[29] Caroline Jansen, "Art Van Furniture files for Chapter 11," *Retail Dive*, March 9, 2020. https://www.retaildive.com/news/art-van-furniture-files-for-chapter-11/573728/.

[30] JC Reindl, "Art Van Furniture files for Chapter 11 bankruptcy, could still face liquidation," *Detroit Free Press*, March 9, 2020. https://www.freep.com/story/money/business/2020/03/09/art-van-furniture-files-bankruptcy/4998785002/.

[31] Frank Witsil, "Art Van Elslander, founder of Art Van Furniture, dies at 87," *Detroit Free Press*, February 12, 2018. https://www.freep.com/story/money/business/2018/02/12/art-van-elslander/329186002/.

[32] Brent Snavely, "A new game, a new life: After facing down alcoholism, Art Van Elslander sets ambitious goals for company," *Crain's Detroit Business*, December 12, 2005. https://www.crainsdetroit.com/article/20180213/news/652806/a-new-game-a-new-life-after-facing-down-alcoholism-art-van-elslander.

[33] Frank Witsil, "Art Van CEO outlines strategy to dominate Midwest furniture sales," *Detroit Free Press*, October 8, 2017. https://www.freep.com/story/money/business/michigan/2017/10/08/art-van-furniture-midwest-michigan/709087001/.

[34] Marianne Wilson, "Midwest furniture chain expands footprint with two family businesses," *Chain Store Age*, November 27, 2017. https://chainstoreage.com/finance-0/midwest-furniture-chain-expands-footprint-two-family-businesses.

[35] Clint Engel, "Blog: Art Van strayed from a clear plan and execution, says former CEO," *Furniture Today*, March 13, 2020, https://www.furnituretoday.com/opinion/clints-notes/blog-art-van-strayed-from-a-clear-plan-and-execution-says-former-ceo/.

[36] Marianne Wilson, "Furniture retailer taps former Barnes & Noble head as CEO," Chain Store Age, April 12, 2018. https://chainstoreage.com/c-suite-1/furniture-retailer-taps-former-barnes-noble-head-ceo.

[37] "Maybe it's not the end for Art Van Furniture after all," *Chicago Business*, March 29, 2020. https://www.chicagobusiness.com/retail/maybe-its-not-end-art-van-furniture-after-all.

[38] Marianne Wilson, *Chain Store Age*.

[39] JC Reindl, "Art Van Furniture to part ways with 2nd CEO since founder's death," *Detroit Free Press*, August 1, 2019. https://www.freep.com/story/money/business/2019/08/01/art-van-ceo-ron-boire-leaving/1891407001/.

[40] JC Reindl, "Art Van Furniture files for Chapter 11 bankruptcy, could still face liquidation," *Detroit Free Press*, March 9, 2020. https://www.freep.com/story/money/business/2020/03/09/art-van-furniture-files-bankruptcy/4998785002/.

[41] Leslie Pappas, "Retail Bankruptcies Leave Consumers Paying Thousands for Nothing," *Bloomberg Law*, April 30, 2020. https://news.bloomberglaw.com/bankruptcy-law/retail-bankruptcies-leave-consumers-paying-thousands-for-nothing.

Chapter 7: Logistics

[1] Dan Cook, "Third-Party Logistics," *IBISWorld*, March 2019. https://www.ibisworld.com/united-states/market-research-reports/third-party-logistics-industry/.

[2] Ibid.

[3] E. Mazareanu, "Coronavirus: impact on the transportation and logistics industry worldwide - Statistics & Facts," *Statista*, June 3, 2020. https://www.statista.com/topics/6350/coronavirus-impact-on-the-transportation-and-logistics-industry-worldwide/.

[4] "XPO Logistics profit tumbled after coronavirus pummeled business," *Reuters*. May 4, 2020. https://www.reuters.com/article/us-xpo-results/xpo-logistics-profit-tumbled-after-coronavirus-pummeled-business-idUSKBN22G2QJ.

[5] "Amazon," *Morningstar*, accessed June 6, 2020. https://www.morningstar.com/stocks/xnas/amzn/quote.

[6] "Amazon Global Supply Chain and Fulfillment Center Network," *MWPVL*, May 17, 2020. https://www.mwpvl.com/html/amazon_com.html.

[7] Spencer Soper, "The man who built Amazon's delivery machine," *Bloomberg*, December 18, 2019. https://www.bloomberg.com/news/articles/2019-12-17/amazon-holiday-shopping-the-man-who-makes-it-happen.

[8] "Amazon Global Supply Chain and Fulfillment Center Network," *MWPVL*.

[9] Joann Muller, "Amazon is gaining on shipping giants," *Axios*, May 29, 2020. https://www.axios.com/amazon-transportation-leaders-c1951c79-2751-489c-98b0-8736e82f0c84.html.

[10] Motley Fool Staff, "How Does XPO Logistics Serve Its Customers?," *Motley Fool*, March 4, 2019. https://www.fool.com/investing/2019/03/04/how-does-xpo-logistics-serve-its-customers.aspx.

[11] "XPO Logistics Again Ranked No. 1 in Transportation and Logistics on Fortune 500," *Global Newswire*, May 19, 2020. https://www.globenewswire.com/news-release/2020/05/19/2035504/0/en/XPO-Logistics-Again-Ranked-No-1-in-Transportation-and-Logistics-on-Fortune-500.html.

[12] "XPO Logistics reports sharp profit drop, pulls 2020 forecasts," *Reuters*, May 4, 2020. https://www.reuters.com/article/xpo-results/xpo-logistics-reports-sharp-profit-drop-pulls-2020-forecasts-idUSL1N2CM15R.

[13] Jamel Toppin, "Better Than Amazon? How Bradley Jacobs Turned A $63M Bet into A $12 Billion Transportation Empire," *Forbes*, April 10, 2018. https://www.forbes.com/sites/antoinegara/2018/04/10/xpo-logistics-bradley-jacobs-billionaire/#ad6f042ca6c4.

[14] Mark B. Solomon, "The big bet of Brad Jacobs," *DC Velocity*, January 9, 2012. https://www.dcvelocity.com/articles/29993-accomplishing-the-impossible-interview-with-brad-jacobs.

[15] Jennifer Smith, "Bradley Jacobs Has Acquired More Than 500 Companies. Here's What He Has Learned," *The Wall Street Journal*, October 27, 2019. https://www.wsj.com/articles/bradley-jacobs-has-acquired-more-than-500-companies-heres-what-he-has-learned-11572228061.

[16] Mark B. Solomon, "Accomplishing the impossible: interview with Brad Jacobs," *DC Velocity*, August 17, 2018. https://www.dcvelocity.com/articles/29993-accomplishing-the-impossible-interview-with-brad-jacobs.

[17] Jamel Toppin, *Forbes*.

[18] Ed Hammond, "XPO Logistics Explores Breakup of Transportation Company, *Bloomberg*, January 15, 2020. https://www.bloomberg.com/news/articles/2020-01-15/xpo-logistics-is-said-to-explore-breaking-up-the-company.

[19] Todd Maiden, "XPO ends bid to break up the company," *Freight Waves*, March 20, 2020. https://www.freightwaves.com/news/xpo-ends-bid-to-break-up-the-company.

[20] "Brad Jacobs and Matt Fassler at the 13th Annual Wolfe Research Global Transportation and Industrials Conference," *Marketscreener*, May 21, 2020. https://www.marketscreener.com/XPO-LOGISTICS-INC-11890333/news/XPO-Logistics-Brad-Jacobs-and-Matt-Fassler-at-the-13th-Annual-Wolfe-Research-Global-Transportation-30651158/.

[21] Brian Kaberline, "Shipping declines send YRC stock downhill," *Kansas City Business Journal*, June 10, 2020. https://www.bizjournals.com/kansascity/news/2020/06/10/yrc-worldwide-shippling-decline-stock-slide.html.

[22] Wallace Witkowski, "YRC Worldwide to effect 1:25 reverse stock split," *MarketWatch*, September 29, 2010. https://www.marketwatch.com/story/yrc-worldwide-to-effect-125-reverse-stock-split-2010-09-29.

[23] William B. Cassidy, "YRC Launches Massive Reverse Stock Split," *Journal of Commerce*, December 1, 2011. https://www.joc.com/trucking-logistics/ltl-shipping/yrc-launches-massive-reverse-stock-split_20111201.html.

[24] Rip Watson, "YRC Chief Zollars to Retire After Recovery Plan Is Done," *Transport Topics*, October 4, 2010. https://www.ttnews.com/articles/yrc-chief-zollars-retire-after-recovery-plan-done.

[25] Claudia H. Deutsch, "No. 2 in Trucking, Yellow, Will Buy No. 1, Roadway," *New York Times*, July 9, 2003. https://www.nytimes.com/2003/07/09/business/no-2-in-trucking-yellow-will-buy-no-1-roadway.html.

[26] "William Zollars of YRC Worldwide: Keep on truckin'," *Institutional Investor*, March 16, 2006. https://www.institutionalinvestor.com/article/b150nr9q6q738j/william-zollars-of-yrc-worldwide-keep-on-truckin.

[27] Rip Watson, *Transport Topics*.

[28] Mark B. Solomon, "YRC to tap James Welch, long-time trucking executive, as new CEO," *DC Velocity*, July 21, 2011. https://www.dcvelocity.com/articles/25511-yrc-to-tap-james-welch-long-time-trucking-executive-as-new-ceo.

[29] David Twiddy, "YRC's Zollars: He would have done few things differently," *Kansas City Business Journal*, July 22, 2011. https://www.bizjournals.com/kansascity/blog/2011/07/yrcs-zollars-he-would-have-done-few.html.

[30] Brian Kaberline, "YRC's new CEO takes the wheel early," *Kansas City Business Journal*, May 7, 2018. https://www.bizjournals.com/kansascity/news/2018/05/07/yrc-s-new-ceo-takes-the-wheel-early.html.

[31] HDT Staff, "YRC Hit by Industrial Slowdown, Makes Leadership Changes," *Trucking Info*, December 13, 2019. https://www.truckinginfo.com/346458/yrc-hit-by-industrial-slowdown-makes-leadership-changes.

[32] David McCann, "Anatomy of a Turnaround: YRC Worldwide," *CFO*, February 10, 2015. https://www.cfo.com/credit/2015/02/anatomy-turnaround-yrc-worldwide/.

[33] Jennifer Smith, "YRC Seeks to Preserve Cash in Troubled Trucking Market," *Wall Street Journal*, May 11, 2020. https://www.wsj.com/articles/yrc-seeks-to-preserve-cash-in-troubled-trucking-market-1158923819.7.

[34] Chris Isidore, "The Trump administration just lent $700 million to a trucking company sued for ripping off taxpayers," *CNN Business*, July 1, 2020. https://www.cnn.com/2020/07/01/business/yrc-federal-loan/index.html.

Chapter 8: Leading Through Strategic Mindset

[1] Peter Cohan, "Amazon's Looming Problem: Who Has the Strategic Mindset to Replace Jeff Bezos?," *Forbes*, June 26, 2020. https://www.forbes.com/sites/petercohan/2020/06/26/amazons-looming-problem-who-has-the-strategic-mindset-to-replace-jeff-bezos/#645bb8c11537.

[2] Peter Cohan, "Startup Cities: Why Only a Few Cities Dominate the Global Startup Scene and What the Rest Should Do About It," (*Apress*: 2018).

[3] Peter Cohan, *Forbes*.

[4] Peter Cohan, "*Forbes*

[5] Peter Cohan, "Five Tests That Your Board Is Doing Its Job," *Inc.*, July 2, 2020. https://www.inc.com/peter-cohan/five-tests-that-your-board-is-doing-its-job.html?cid=sf01001.

[6] Ibid.

[7] "Our History," *Walmart.com*, accessed July 10, 2020. https://corporate.walmart.com/our-story/our-history.

[8] Brittain Ladd, "What If General George Patton Was the CEO of Walmart?," *Observer*, July 29, 2019. https://observer.com/2019/07/walmart-ecommerce-strategy-amazon-ceo-george-patton/.

[9] Peter Cohan, *Inc.*

[10] Based on Peter Cohan, "Scaling Your Startup," *Apress*: 2019, Chapter 9.

I

Index

P. S. Cohan, *Goliath Strikes Back*, https://doi.org/10.1007/978-1-4842-6519-2

D

E

F

G, H

I, J, K

L, M

N

O

P, Q

R, S

T

U

V

W

Y, Z

Made in the USA
Middletown, DE
28 February 2021

34545979R10110